A Daily Poem touched by Heaven

A Daily Poem touched by Heaven

Cathy E. Hodgson

authorHOUSE®

AuthorHouse™
1663 Liberty Drive
Bloomington, IN 47403
www.authorhouse.com
Phone: 1-800-839-8640

Published by AuthorHouse   07/18/2012

ISBN: 978-1-4772-0875-5 (sc)
ISBN: 978-1-4772-0876-2 (hc)
ISBN: 978-1-4772-0877-9 (e)

Library of Congress Control Number: 2012909364

CONTENTS

Chapter 1

Chapter 2

Chapter 3

Chapter 4

Chapter 5

Chapter 6

Chapter 7

Chapter 8

Chapter 9

Chapter 10

Chapter 11

Chapter 12

FOREWORD

You are holding in your hands a marvelous gift of inspiration, faith and joy—a collection of poems—one for each day of the year—that will delight, inspire and sustain you as you face your own challenges in your life.

The poems run the gamut of the whole of human experience—from the simple joys and happiness of just being alive and a part of a world larger than oneself to complex issues of temptation, sin and forgiveness and the tests one's own faith and belief in God often meet.

The true value of any great book can be measured in how one feels after having read it. Did it inspire, give encouragement or provide some form of joy? With this book you are sure to be spiritually refreshed and invigorated after having read it.

The poems of this volume are like so many pearls on a beautiful necklace. Individually, each can be enjoyed for its own merits, but collectively they comprise something that is greater than the sum of its parts.

Don Odom

Wawarsing, NY

ACKNOWLEDGMENTS

I want to thank the love of my life, my husband, Michael Hodgson for his support in my work.

I would like to thank my daughter, Amber D. Roby for her time editing, and layout design of this book.

I would like to thank my amazing friend, Jane Frisby for her time proofreading, editing and her

help with scripture references for the poems.

I want to thank all my poetry friends for the encouragement and time spent reading my work.

REVIEWS

Cathy Hodgson is a writer of light . . . the light of love,
her book, "A Poem a Day Touched by Heaven",
Acknowledges God as the creator of all life
including nature's beauty. She knows that if
one listens closely with their heart, nature
speaks in its own language. When nature
speaks, its God speaking asking for our
acknowledgment of His love.
Her writing is evidence of her spirituality.

Elizabeth Durney Publisher," My World in Poetry."

A book of poetry that will take you from one extreme to the next,
Some will make you laugh and some will make you cry . . . . and some
will make you realize most people have almost the same feelings as you
do . . . . a very good must read book.

Jane Frisby Editor/proof reader

Beautiful work is shared when she writes her heart fills and auras bound.
It takes you her world of light, love the way she shares her words it
touches my heart each time! She inspires!

Deborah Shepard author of "The Pages of Time"

A fantastic poetry writer, Alma Wicker

CHAPTER 1

Happy New Year

Yet

Another year

One that promises

A new song beginning

Don't look back with regret

But yet maybe with love eyes

Sing the songs that whispers joy

In the heart deep you know

A true one that sings soft

Like the lamb, nudging

Nibbling to hum

Peaceful

Quiet

Joy

Deep

Inspired

You know

The songs tune

So go on and dance

Happy New Year!

Hebrews 12:2

Busting Butt

Like a cat that's had her cream

One wants to curl up and dream

When the belly is full and round

Yet dreams won't lose a pound

Get now go out and walk

I know! I know! Don't bulk!

A lot of this is idol talk

Lord, don't let me sulk

Off to take a break

I'll see what's at stake

I want to fit in smaller clothes

I want it easy to touch my toes

So bust my butt I must

Put them tracks in the dust

I am willing to give my most

So I don't feel so gross.

1 Corinthians 6:19 & 20

Hooked

How easy to be brought into your seductive words . . .

Words that race through the mind

Making me think of things forbidden . . .

Thoughts that lure me from true love . . .

Thoughts that bring me in Satan's arms!

There would be pleasure,

The body would cry with pleasure,

I know this because,

I have been caught in this snare,

Trapped unable to move . . .

Should I . . . Could I . . .

Would I . . .

Throw away my very soul,

For this fleeting temptation?

Selling my very soul, for the such?

Turning apart, is not easy,

But separate, I must . . .

To end this lure, this lust.

Yet, have I not, been raped

In mind . . .

Matthew 26:41

Chains

There are walls that bind the hands and feet

Caged in by chains that grasp the mind

A dictator of lost dreams, the exterminator

Of fruition, the prognosticator of deception

Pray this demon elude you,

That the gift of message,

Be fresh, flowing and prosper you

That your dreams would travel freely

Psalm 73:6

Acts 12

Growing Prayer

Precious Heavenly Father

Who is, was and is to come

Humbly, I bow my lowly head

I kiss Holy feet with lips of despair

My soul is tarnished

Unworthy to be in Your presence

Yet, do I come

You reach down

Fold me in Your arms

Cloak me in Your shining robe

I melt at Your holiness

Your agape love overwhelms

How do I get such faith?

Belief that will move my mountains

Thomas is my brother

May I touch Your nail scared hands?

Only to wish I did not

Faith, to only believe

Take me to that growing place

That I may be nourished

That my mustard seed

Might find fertile ground to grow . . .

Amen

Psalm 95:6

The Quest

I step in place

The digits go wild!

The numbers flash

Saying anything but mild!

My mind blows

My eyes bulge

This gadget is broke!

Why must I indulge!

It's simple to say

A quest must be made

I'll step up again in 365 days

This debt must be paid!

Romans 8:18-23

Prisoner of Snow

Shadows close over night

Universe ends by darkness

Wind rises to flow with breath

But time on earth has passed

I have seen dawn's meeting

In stretch watched lonely moon

Wrestled myself to see vision

Bliss is heaven walking shore

Airless tide rolls in and out

To quench entwined stars

Nature beats flowing sorrow

Stinging heart grows limp

Light increases spasm to dimness

By soft voice I whisper dream

Slumber over takes a lone heart

Yet sun would not melt the snow

Revelation 22:5

Trying out my new snow shoes

It started as a trip to the grocery store.
I had to turn around,
I couldn't get through the door
That wasn't the worst of this awful tale.

I fell over the hand rail!
It was at the football game.
I was traveling down the hall.
I went to buy myself the biggest coke,
that is how my clothes got soaked.

Don't tell my husband about the car
I don't think it will go very far!
My feet got stuck on the accelerator,
off I zoomed like an elevator!
Then I went through an open door
It went all the way to my heater core!

When I tried to get out of the car
I was setting at the bar
I may not look real fit
But I still have some of my wit . . .
I knew it was time for me to split
When the seat of pants went rip
But someone handed me a drink
That's all that happened, I think?
I have such a big head ache

Don't think I'll wear those shoes again,
For my own and my marriage sake!!

Psalm 85:8

14

Touch me in the Morning

Touch me in the morning
Touch me when I close my eyes
Bring to me your presence
As through my life I walk

Dance with me in gladness
Cry with me in pain
Be by my side in sorrow
All through my life you reign

Sing for me exalted
Above the valley low
Look down to this mere mortal
Bless me as I go

I'll praise you on the mountain
Because I love you so
No matter what's in tomorrow
Onward together we'll go
Touch me in the morning
Touch me when I close my eyes
Bring to me your presence
As through my life I walk

Isaiah 58:8

Winter Dreams

When cold winds of winter blow
When they stop I long to know
The cold fills my weathered bone
I am so glad I am at home

I burrow down under my covers
While friends are sunshine lovers
I dream of words that hug my brow
The wisdom is my marrow pal

It is a ghost from long ago
Ancient writers I long to know
Scratching pictures in the stone
The pen and ink is mine alone

They must have felt it through their skin
Flowing through their primitive pen
A need to flow in measured beat
Written down forever to keep

Oh, ghost of writers gone before
Fill my dreams with lovely lore
Keep them tangled in my mind
That way I will always find

The words to form from my pen
Visions of how it must have been
The haunts of those before even you
Before the creation that heaven knew

Psalm 74:16 & 17

The Last War, Armageddon

The Last War, Armageddon
The slanted eyes green and cold

Face the others light blue and bold
Black feathers rose for intent

White ones flash forward and bent
Circling one another on angry ground

Wishing the other dead and bound
A sword is drawn from a golden sheath

A silver one brought from underneath
Black and white wings wisp with flair

Feathers flying through the air
Blood drips to the cold ash floor

No time to stop or there will be more
The air is charge with the fight

Metal clicking through the night
Around about a crowd has flew

To watch until a life is through

For this fight is more than seen

It's a fight for a new world King

For in the scrolls of ancient old

A fight of brazen evil was foretold

Armageddon its Bible name

Things will never be the same

They both know who is told will win

But he will never quit his blacken sin

Blackened evil runs through his vein

He will never relent the reign

Then a sword flung to the ground

The breath silence all around

Instead of being struck through the heart

He was bound and made to part

In a place of pit and fire

Cast forever to burn and sire

Rev 16:16

18

I Am Leaving

When that trumpet sounds

I won't be around

I'm going to split this place

For I'll have won the race!

I'll run right pass that gate

To the loving arms that wait!

Please don't play with fate

You might be too late!

It is a joyous ending

With Christ ascending

So please don't stall

Because heaven will call!

Revelation 22:3-7

God's Love

I had to hit the bottom.
Before I would call . . .
So you could pick me up . . .
Why did I have to fall?

No one would come here
Here in this ravine
I was so desperate,
Cold, lone, afraid . . .

I didn't know you were there
You see how I needed you.
When I didn't know you
Were even there . . .

Then you showed yourself to me . . .
In your eyes all I could see was love.
I was down in this bottom
Where friends wouldn't come

I lay here dying
Without any to love me
All I could see was destitute.
No hope was there for me.

You stretched out a hand
Your love I could feel
Down in this the bottom
Where friends wouldn't come . . .

Psalm 40:2-3

Deceiving Sun

The light emitting from the sun,
Seem to radiate heat
But don't let your heart skip a beat
It's a sunny delusional deceit

The temp ridged and cold
One has to be bold
Should listen to what's told
To stay in from this blistering cold

Frost Stings the finger tips
Light rays glisten from the sun
Feeling like little rips
Too cold to have any fun

Padded feet to the porch floor
Dredging through the snow
Can't wait to get to the door
But hit the ice and down I go

Sliding on the porch
And right through the door
The fire place feels like a torch
Yet it warms my feet so sore

Isaiah 4:6

21

The Trail of Ice Queens

White Fairy dust

glitters like diamonds.

The sun dances in the sky

spreading its glittering wand.

The hills and trees rise

to meet enchanting sparkles.

The trail of ice queens

are laid about the land.

It makes for

an eye rendering sight

That burst with beauty

Fit for a King . . .

Psalm 51:7

If the Moon failed to Shine

If the moon failed to shine,

A star would forget to twinkle

Would love find love without enchantment?

Would heart grow dim without a light to whisper?

Rain would have its way in heaven

Clouds would clap and flash like war

Dampness and cold would be the night

The reaper would raise his sword for death

Would angels still travel on earthly soil?

If the moon failed to shine

Psalm 72:7

My Lovers

I walk into the room,
I am attacked with so much love,

My legs are tangled with his,
I can hardly walk.

I put my hand out,
it is met with an unimaginable softness.

She smooth's her body so close,
it takes me aback.

I brush my fingers through her long hair,
so soft, I can feel the fast beat of her heart.

He is lying between my feet, warm and asleep,
but I only think this, he winks up at me!

She massages my body,
the kind of massage that leaves you in awe!

Unconditional love, you bet!

Finally my loves are alert,
as I open their can of Tuna!

Jeremiah 31:3

Winter Wonderland

Snow covered hills
And frosted trees
Snowflakes blowing
In the breeze

Oh what a winter wonderland
Void of oceans summer sand

Crystal diamonds
In the sun
White frosted breath
Shown on the run

Bitten toes and bright red nose
When winter wonderland breath blows

Thick bright socks
To warm your feet
Small comforts
In winters feat

Warmth from the fireplace
Coco makes the cold blood race

All wrapped up in God's plan
This season of the earth
By His mighty hand
In this winter wonderland

Psalm 33:8-9

Faithful Morning

Yet the night dreams embrace with grace

From the dew sparkling emerald on the leaf

Heart whispers holding shiny light

Yet awake morn to see suns gifting rays

Magnificence will unfold throughout time

Breeze flows in constant warming touch

Blooms rarity sings true grace as angelica

Heavens light dances through time remembering

Kissing by the shores of yesterday's whispers

Heart would be heavy to hold her days dreamt

But the sky folds each into her bosomed cloud

Dancing to each keepsake like it was yesterday

Oh time, keep your hand away from dream

It will need to live with no lasting sorrow

Let it spring to the green faithful as dawn.

Lamentations 3:22-23

Flavored Ice Cream

Every morning let the sunshine on my face

Even if the gray clouds fill the space

There is always something to look forward to

Look for the flowers don't be staying blue

Every morning it's a disgrace

What the shadows do to my face

I'm going to learn to change my own

Like a flavored ice cream cone

I'm gonna dance until I smile

Even if it takes a little while

I'll spread some joy around

No more blues to be found

1 Thessalonians 5:18

It Wasn't a Dream

Love whispers through my hair
soft rustling from your lips
faint smell of smoked wood
feeling warmth of your body

Touching fingers entwined mine
sending flutters to heart
closed eyes relish the moment
taken away in your love

Soaring to your beating heart
like a ballerina on her tips
dampness moistens open lips
my eyes burn glassy with heat

I am lost in your aurora
tumbling I fall to indistinct
stumbling through a haze
Waking alone

I close my eyes
Trying to capture
that which was lost
No . . . It wasn't a dream

Love whispers through my hair
soft rustling from your lips
faint smell of smoked wood
feeling warmth of your body

I close my eyes
Trying to capture
that which was lost
No . . . it can't be, a dream

Job 20:8

28

The Rush

He was in a hurry as he turned the corner
She couldn't be late her boss had warned her
She hit the wall of mass manly muscle
Oh my! He hit someone hard in his hustle

Long hair sprayed everywhere as she hit the floor
He should have been watching as he soars
He moves the silk to see her face
Was she harmed, there was no trace

Long full lashes opened to a flutter
Something in his gut turned to butter
Crystal gray eyes looked into his face
His heart stopped, then started to race

Passion Pink lips began to pout
He reached for her, his arm strong and stout
She was confused but took hold of his hand
Wobbled a bit as she tried to stand

His arms were about her in a dash
He was under her spell in the same flash
He brought those passion pink lips up to kiss
Something wasn't right he was amiss

Surprised he was when her lips held secure
He was sure he couldn't take this more allure
They parted and gasp catching their breath
Knowing they would be ever after till death

Ecclesiastes 9:11

Black Feather

I found a Black Feather today . . .

It brought me in thought,

with its presence.

What is this to me?

Is it from a war I can't see?

Is there a war?

being fought for me?

Another realm, could there be?

Images of warriors,

dance in my head.

By the looks,

one soon to be dead!

Images of warriors,

strong and in flight!

Images of warriors,

both strong and in fight!

Images of warriors,

One Dark,

One Light . . .

Ephesians 6:12

Winter's Claim

The northern winds kissed the breeze
There it howled like a ghost whispering
Ice chips danced on the frozen ground
Twirling and swirling its armed apparition
The meager light hardly filtering gray clouds

The new day was here to meet the mind
Filtering what it may bring to humanity
The prince set on his throne indecisive
Where would he turn in this entire blizzard?
The snow made mountains and rivers

The doom spit on her filthy ragged sleeve
The weathered ash face hung and coughed
The warm street vent already taken
Wishing she had got there first
Walking on to a park bench to bed

There would be no stiff bones by morn
Hoping for the relief to come quickly
The midnight bell chimed harsh drama
A lone angel stepped forward intent
Walking down the middle of the street

There was nothing here for him
The other had already laid claim
He heard their parting howls
A single white snowflake danced
Touching his long sodden face

Job 37:5-6
Songs of Solomon 4:16

I Let You Fly

On winters wing I let you fly

Higher than a snowflake sky

Then I went on with my life.

Yet I had a dream you see

That someday you'd come back to me

I watched, wondered and resigned

O the long for passing time

For to ordain an impending sign

That my heart could someday find

The chance to come your way again

Yet of your love, the fate to win

Matthew 6:9-10

Luke 22:41-42

Cold Weather

Here you come from the north

I knew you would to capture me

With chills to the bone

Throwing about icy clouds of moisture

Running away the Sun with gray

Temperature being taken by you

To a dungeon of despair

I am tortured

I want to crawl back

in my fetal position

Where dreams stay

Chasing butterflies in the Sun

Genesis 8:22

Job 37:5-13

Made By God

God took five long days to form and create

Each He spoke and there it was, stars, moon, sun, solar system,

the earth, living animal and everything there in

On the sixth day He came down to earth taking a man like form

Kneeling in the dirt he had made, He gathered the very dust from the ground

In His omnipotent hands he took that dust, mixed it with the sweat of His brow,

Formed each characteristic part, shaping it with his fingertips

Then raising this formation tenderly loving to His mouth

Gave of it His very breath, naming His creation man, made in his image

He lovingly smiled at all His work and rested on the seventh day.

Genesis 1:27

Snow Globe by God

God shook my world today
He took it into both His hands
Shook it, creating a blizzard
Snow whirled around blinding

It came with a brisk violent wind
Whiting out my view of everything
Whisking away my well laid plans
Lost I couldn't see where to go

But then, I looked up,
I watching enchanted,
The snow gentled
Kissing my cheeks and lips
With a thirst quenching moisture

The sun came over the horizon
Touching each flake with a diamond
I watched gems touch the ground
Glistening to sparkle His beauty . . .

It captivated my heart to grow
With a love beyond words
I know through all of my storms
If I can remember to look up

I'll see gems,
made by Gods own hands
He holds the world
by His fingertips.

Psalm 107:29

Thy Gift

Take my hand

With pen inserted

Use thy gift

To write thy words

Holy ink to flow from quill

Writing of thy precious will

Use this word to edify Thee

The more of you and less of me

Give me strength to hear your voice

Writing of your loving choice

Calm the one that is me

Lord I meditate on Thee

So all in all

Of friends and foe

Of your love

I can bestow

Job 32:8

Howling Lone

The quiet of the night mocks my wretched song

The lone path is long winding and shadowy dark

Listen to the howling wolf; he too hides in brush alone

No fanged mate to share his captured bleeding meal

Tarring the flash with teeth snarling at no opponent

I walk on trembling in sorrow tread barren depths

The shaded tree tops hoot with flapping wings

I flinch, withering immovable scared stark stiff

Yet I know I must climb out of this ravine gully

But hence there is little light here to saunter the route

I curl back the paisley coverlet only to coldness

Heart furls snaked in nostalgic repressed images

I pull over the same covering, curling a fetal position

Hoping to bite the dream of a different existence

Psalm 91:15-16

The Dowry

Where is this Hell

Where young female Perish

Not enough wealth to pay

Does love need dowry?

To seal a heart of clay

Oh evil man does

This deed

Nor is it bless by God

For cursed forever and a day

To them that be at odd

Watch young girl

And guard your heart

For love is love of true

For some the deed is only wealth

Make sure the love is true.

Dedicated to the women of India

Galatians 3:13

CHAPTER 2

While you're sleeping

While you're sleeping

I tap out keys

Writing what the mind sees

Will it be some sad muse?

Maybe an inspiration

Someone can use

My eyes so weary

But sleep eludes

I set and ponder the write

Hoping for some divine insight

Praying for anointing to ring

With something enlighten to bring

But all I have is sleepy rambling

A mind so tired all is scrambling

I'll just close my eyes a bit

It might bring a little wit

Soon the dreams of sleep invade

The need to write with them fades

Songs of Solomon 5:2

Shant Care!

Awe my chickadee,

What a delight to see you.

Fluttering here at my window,

Your song brings a smile.

My day shall be bright,

The candle you have lit.

I will reflect as I work,

Your voice so fair.

Associates will wonder,

In step and stare.

But I shant care,

what is.

I have in my heart a tune,

Fluttering on the wing.

A melody that is written,

Only for me!

Isaiah 5:1

People Need You Lord

I climb to the mountain top with you by my side
I tread through the valley with you as my guide

I whisper to you a prayer
My heart knows you are there

People need you Lord
I know that you care

Soften their hearts
To hear your soft voice

If they could just listen
They would rejoice

We don't have to go on alone
Though the hurt is our own

You'll give us a shoulder to cry on,
a hand to hold tight

You tell us you love us,
That you'll take on our fight

We must believe in you
With all of our might

As we travel this journey
It's better with you,
on our flight

Matthew 11:28-30

Before the Rooster Cry

The steam from the tea kettle
cast shadows on the wall
The juice from the orange
dripped slowly and began to fall

She wiped her chin softly
as if someone would see
She filled the dainty pot
with water for her tea

She rushed to her pad and pen
with her muse flying free
Inking her flowing flights
before the muse would flee

It started with an inkling
somewhere in back of her mind
with a growing sense it intrigued her
to form a rhyme

All before the morning sunshine
would brighten the eastern sky
She had a poem written
before the rooster would cry

Psalm 46:5

Leftovers

I feel you close in this room

Looking out for my best

I feel you here but far away

Wishing you'd come back to stay

I feel the love

You have for me

In that land of between

Beyond that place not human seen

Helping till my calling day

The day I will meet you there

In that far heavenly land

When the angel takes my hand

Or is it just left over love

Some aura from above

Angels, some would say

Left to help, till my dying day

Psalm 16:11

45

Snowed In

I watch a single snowflake float by
then others fall from the sky
I watch out my window in awe
as they increase and multiply

Now the sky is all most all white
this is such a beautiful sight
Even more seems to take flight
till nothing but powdering white

I open my door to a wall of snow
full of snowflakes all in a row
Husband! Come see this snow
but all he does is stub his toe!

This is what it is like be snowed in
no way to get to friends or kin
Forget about moving your car
If you can find it won't go far!

Job 38:22, Psalm 51:7

Moon Set

The stillness of the cold

makes my breath, a mist in white

The Moon set this morn

makes the sky very light . . .

The sun coming up from the east

makes the shadows run away

This early a day . . .

the cold it creeps in my fingers

Like a demon of stone . . .

But the artist can't resist.

The painting

that's being sewn . . .

Job 40:10

Letting Go

It's sad to see a friendship die

Sometimes there is nothing

You can do . . .

You try to take the time

But they turn their back on you

It leaves you with a forlorn hurt

An empty place of void . . .

But people change and so does love

Sometimes it's for the best

When all goes hand in hand

True love will stand the test

Romans 12:19

Through the Door

The proximity of his words quickens my breath
It strangles my inner bowels
I am lost like a sheep gone astray
I cry to be held by loving arms lost to me

Waves of ocean cool my heated feet
Bubbling up to the misty breeze
I daze as the rising sun shimmers
Prisms of tiny rainbows, like fairies dancing

Heaven help me, I am lost to all reality
My mind sways to and fro with the breeze
Touching sometimes on ecstatic then atrocious
The bipolar of emotions are set aside

Smiles play my silly face I listen to his song
On the wings of a dove twittering the low limb
I close my eyes and hear his voice
Strong and bold yet gently mild

The dream takes me to my happy place
I pull tight the imagined cloak
Wrapping myself in this dream
Wishing to get lost in Heaven
Through the door to not return!

Hosea 2:15

Looking Silly

When your presence came into the room,

I knew I would be doomed . . .

With your presence you bowled me over,

for you I would roll over and play dead!

Or catch a stick, just like you said!

Snap your fingers, I would prance,

I sure enjoyed for you to dance!

For me it worked out just fine.

Because for you, it was the same,

for me your wolf was tame!

This thing we have probably looks silly!

But we are both so willing!

Matthew 26:31

Psalm 110:3

Cupid's Arrow

I've been hit by my own arrow
Will I be a victim to this folly?
How could this make me jolly?
The blood how it seeps
from my wound
All I do is swoon
Like some silly
School aged kid in this dilly
My words won't form
from my lips they are torn
Shy I've never been
This psyche can I win
I must run to my closest kin
You've turn me outward in
Maybe I'll just die
I shake my head to sigh
Why of this arrow
Must I show
Surrender with a bow
this wound runs deep
But true to self I'll keep
then you walk by
If I could just play the lie
I'll just follow you
to the end
of, of
the
world . . . .

Psalm 11:1-2

51

Chocolate Dreams

While good love is nice
Sometimes the man I will ditch!
I want something Rich . . .
When only chocolate I kiss!
Nuts are an option.

But more chocolate is best.
I could leave the rest!
with whip cream
to fill this dream!

I might have it Hot
with marshmallows on top!

Dark chocolate soufflés
with cream anglaise . . .
Brings a moan to my mouth
and is sure to amaze!

But just for this need,
Chocolate's the lead
Oreo cookies crumbed up fine
with chocolate cheese cake,
with chocolate chips!
Are in line!

Ephesians 2:3

Be Mine

I glance into her eyes of blue
Wonder why no one captured you
wishing I could make you mine
If only I could find the right line

Oh, he turns and looks my way
I wonder what words I can say
I need a time of extension
That I can capture his attention

Oh the dream, that she'd see me
I'd kneel right now, on bended knee
All I can do is look to the floor
She steps away toward to door

I bat my eyes and look his way
Trying to find some word to say
I throw my long hair over my shoulder
Hoping the gesture makes him bolder

Knowing this is my last chance
I think I'll ask her to dance
I straighten myself and take a step
I find that the floor is quite wet

What happen next is still a blur

I really am still not quite sure

I ran to see him all in a scramble

On the floor in a shamble

Displayed on the floor in the room

Looking like a great big goon

But then it is her who kneels

Is it a dream, my mind it reels

His head I shelter in my lap

What an awful mishap

His eyes they look off too far

I think he is a little ajar

The concern that mirrors in baby blues

Could make a tale for a poet to use

My heart she has captured in her hand

I think I hear the angel band

Then the smile over takes his face

Oh it makes my heart to race

He looks up and says I'll be fine

If you'll just promise to be mine!

John 15:16-19

His Love

She seen the light of him standing there
But thought, for me Christ could not care
I mess this life up all the time
He's here for some one more sublime

But his hand was outstretched
She felt like she was such a wretch
She turned to see if someone else was there
It couldn't be for her He'd care

As soon as his hand touched her skin
She became aware of all her sin
The sobs escaped from somewhere in her heart
It's OK; I'll take them, sin now part

She watched as blood like sweat ran from his face
She knew then He'd died to save her a place
Someday I'll take you home with me
But there are still those who need set free

With that message, He was gone
She knew then she must continue on
To share the love she'd found that day
So for on earth now she would stay

John 3:16
John 15:13

The Morning

The night air has kissed,

the morning with dew.

The sun on the horizon,

is lighting the sky blue.

A glisten from the moisture,

reflects like a jewel.

The soft caw of a bird,

as she searches for her love

The dove in the tree,

says good morning from above.

The water reflecting,

The beauty around

By His artistic hand

You are astounded!

Sets the scene for the morning

So tranquil a gift.

For this kind of setting.

Gives the heart such a lift

Isaiah 58:8

Until Next Time We Meet

I bow my head call your name

I know you hear

I close my eyes

There's no need

You are always there

I love the closeness

That it brings

To say a heartfelt prayer

I come into your presence

knowing that you care

I empty my burdens

You hear them everyone

I know you listen

Though I ramble on

Somehow my heart is lifted

You've reached down your hand

Pulled me to my feet

I can take on come what may

Until next time we meet

Psalm 5:3

Should I Not Be Jealous

Should I not be jealous of your folly?

You now dance with angel wings

High in the sky

Bouncing on soft clouds lined with gold

While I here below toil to make a buck

To feed bread to my hungry mouth

While, ha, there you are

With your Manna sweet bread feasting

With the God Prince

Should I not be jealous?

That you have no more pain

Nor despair, Ever!

You left me!

In this land of snow,

rain and then the heat

To fear to die

I don't want to go on

Should I be jealous of you?

Going on without me!

I miss you . . .

Matthew 5:4

58

Seasons

Dreaming of another day
On my way to work

The sun just peeped over the horizon
Birthing another day to lurk

I dream of another kind
Not one at the grime

One I can take snapping pictures
watching a lone cloud float by

Skipping rocks across the creek
Going for a run until I'm beat

Watching leaves flutter in autumn
Watching the snow sprinkling winter

Sniffing the buds of new spring
The butterflies flutter in summer

But all this is a dream
Just a dreamers dream . . .

Genesis 1:14
Ecclesiastes 3:1

Now I Can't Go

It was a quite Eve,
with a soft eastern breeze.
The Sun had just begun to set in the east.
Making shadows deep on the ground.

We were getting ready
to relax for the night
after a busy day,
the two of us.

You were in the bath
shaving, I could hear the
small buzz of the motor.

I thought over yesterday,
How you wanted me to go to church.
With you, but I wouldn't.

I said some day
it will be a surprise for you.
The sad look in your eyes
tore my heart for a moment.

I don't know why I wouldn't go
I just couldn't.
It seems to be your passion
lately . . .

The buzz was still going
on in the bath . . .
I rose to have a look!

You are my men attractive
vibrant, alive with passion,
for whatever you do!
I look in the door . . .

The razor is hanging from its cord!
But you are not there!
I stare in fear.
I call your name!
But you are not here!

I go out the front door!
You are not there!
I know I will not find you!!
But I keep looking!

Getting more frantic as I go!
Exhausted! I fall!!
I know I have been left!
I didn't heed the call . . .

Now I can't go!!!

Matthew 24:36-51

Wondering

I wonder of the companionship we share.
I love you; I feel so close to you now.

But a while ago with you my heart began to tear.
I just wonder what happened there.

I know I didn't dream it.
You just were not with me.

I just couldn't see where you could be?
Unattached definitely,

But that time has passed.
I want this feeling to last.

But sometime my mind wonders back.
What was going on, what did we lack?

Should I leave it alone?
Let it remain unknown . . .

I don't want to go back there.
I want to stay as we are right here.

Malachi 3:6

Shelter in a Storm

Jesus had no place of his own

No place to hang a hat

Wandering city to city

To do what God willed

He traveled earth's beauty

Meeting people with open hearts

Many miracles were preformed

Most would call Him a Nomad

In His book inspiring words

Lay not your treasures here

It's hard to do, its society

To build your own castle

But lay your burden at His feet

Him who traveled without a home

He will bring you needed shelter

In times of every storm

Philippians 4:13

The Unimportant Human Girl

I look to the heavens; they seem so close
I think of the magnificence, how vast it is

Does he really care
for someone way down here?

A dream like scene passes by,
with all the imagined tales

The cloud moves with a mellow dance
opening heaven's window for a glance

It goes on the distance to fade
As my eyes slumber to close

I dream of walking Streets of gold
Oh the stories I've been told

But does he really know me
This unimportant human girl

As I turn, his eyes meet mine
Then I know it all is fine

He walks to me,
His arms out stretched

I feel the words that are unsaid
He's been waiting all this time

I feel His warm tear drop
I love you so much,

my precious dear.

Jeremiah 1:5

Dreams of Tomorrow

The grass tickles my feet
As barefoot we walk
We spread a blanket
To set and talk

I'll lay my head on your shoulder
As we dream of the life
We'll soon have together
When I become your wife

We'll have a little cottage up on the hill
Making love whenever we will
We won't wait long, children to bear
Your blue eyes, blond hair like mine and fair

I'll tend to my rose garden
While you work through the day
When you're home in the evening
We'll take time to play

When you leave in the morning
We'll hate to part
But while you're away,
You'll be in my heart

Isaiah 62:5

The Kiss

Kisses play against silken temple

Whispering the hearts endearment

Breathe sizzling against soft skin

Tracing moist face in tiny caresses

In a quest to find lips to sate

Pressing snug to parted lips

Lips that are rendered helpless

The headiness' rips seamless

The heart beats a tune building

Tongue enters its tomb

Diving the depth rendering lost

Blood runs molten though the veins

Kissing each nerve to erupt fire

Sizzling with argue of sanity

To leash the action on hold

Pants for air break

The bearer apart

Eyes glisten into another deep

Holding in question

Songs of Solomon 1:2

Twinkle in my Eyes

Stars how they twinkle in my eyes
As I think of the Moon so high

Playing on the wings of the wind
Flying to this splendid song
Oh, oh, there isn't a thing wrong
This melody so sweet to me

Love like this there's never been
Oh, Dear God don't let it end
We laughed at the rainbow in the sky
Strumming colors at the end of a storm

Can you see, can't you see
How this love was born
It started as friends you and me
Never will it fade away
They'll be blue skies in everyday

Stars how they twinkle in my eyes
As I think of the Moon so high

Songs of Solomon 4:16

Job 19:27

Love Kissed Muse

I walk on the shore of your muse

Enchanted by the kiss that lingers

You take me dreaming in mysteries

I dance on the tips of my high heel shoes

I sway to the rhyme and rhythm with breeze

The sweet scent of heavenly orchids

Reaches touching twilight misty stars

The owl watches wide eyed at the twilights

That reflects in our florescent locked eyes

Loves halo an aurora enlightens our path

The music goes on like a symphony

Forever an eternity of love kissed muse

Psalm 30:11

Jeremiah 31:13

How much do you love me?

Here I am, it's me
Take my timid hand
Sweet heart, I am here
Deep in heart I feel you

You are always there
Two hearts like one
Every minute I think
I think of you

How much do you love me?
I feel how you do
Whispering in tune
Oh, the stars how they bloom

Take me dear
Forgive me a friend
There is no other
Let us go hand and hand

Mysteries happen
I don't understand
But it won't be denied
It's what I feel inside

How much do you love me?
I feel how you do
Whispering in tune
Oh, the stars how they bloom

How much do you love me?
Here I am it's me
Take my timid hand
Sweet heart, I am here

Deep in heart I feel you
You are always there
Two hearts like one
Every minute I think

I think of you
How much do you love me?
I feel how you do
Whispering in tune

Oh, the stars how they bloom
Take me dear
Forgive me a friend
There is no other

Let us go hand and hand
Mysteries happen
I don't understand
But it won't be denied

It's what I feel inside
How much do you love me?
I feel how you do
Whispering in tune
Oh, the stars how they bloom

Psalm 91:14
John 21:15-17

Leap Day Quest

She waited while watching the days

Each February day her palms sweat

More nervousness growing each day

Would he accept her daring plight?

Oh my! She only had one mere day!

One day in four years to get it right . . .

She read the ancient fables and tales

How the ladies ran to catch a man

Sighing she also read, some hid off

Not wanting caught in the scheme

He had told her how he loved her

It was not a rambunctious dream!

But the question, was she a fool

To take the next step this time

Her quest strayed knees trembled

Oh! Oh! The ramblings in her mind

She prayed the good Lords blessing

Was leap year day the right time?

1 Chronicles 28:9

Jeremiah 29:13

CHAPTER 3

The Third Moon

The Lion stretches out his claws,

He roars from winter sleep

The white rain tumbles down

To grasp the cold to keep

The sun rises and tries to help

But she's so far away

A tear falls from her eye

She births its golden ray

A gentle Ba, Ba is heard

As the Lamb is born

The Lion roars his last grip

From his throne he's torn

Revelation 5:5-6

Lost Muse

Where are you muse

What kinda words can I use

Please come take me away

To an awesome land far away

Maybe you will bring, words of love

Something inspirational, from above

Maybe something witty or funny

Maybe joyful or sunny

I know you are in hiding

But I have so much riding

On this God given gift

Truly you are my lift

You have your own personality

Come on, spread your vitality

Deuteronomy 30:14

Romans 10:8

Lost In the Call

Lost in the call

The darkness surrounds

I hear them coming

The evil that bounds

The horned one

Has tempted

Won a little battle

But won't win the war

The white horse is saddled

Ready to ride

At his appearing

No one can hide

Please listen to the calling

That you won't be late

Once he is here

That will be fate

1 Corinthians 15:51-54

Matthew 24: 36

Diamond

I'm your diamond in the rough
Do what you need, mold my stuff

Chip away the limestone shell
Work until all is well

Curving and carving to atone
Make me a treasure all my own

I want to sparkle by your hand
To be a jewel worth a grand

Here on earth a treasured loan
A diamond to shine you have sown

Malachi 3:17

In The Storm

The tears fall like rain

Wish I could take away your pain

The loss is so severe

All I can do is tear

The storms took

For some everything

Some now fly

With angel wings

I bow my head

To say a prayer

Only God knows

How much I care.

Psalm 107:29

Whisper in My Ear

Whisper in my ear . . .
Tell me you are there.

A soft breeze blew
But you didn't hear . . .

Show me in the sky . . .
If you are way up high . . .

The lightening flashed right by
You shook your head to sigh.

Show me in this life . . .
You heard a baby cry . . .

You stopped to ponder.
Could God be just a lie?

Show me some kinda sign.
A crocus peeps through the snow.

I sent you all of this,
But you still didn't know.

1 Kings 19:11-13

Oh Father

Oh Father,

Who is above all?

Who cares beyond heaven for us?

I bow a humble head to you,

I asked you to care for your hurting people.

Many have traveled countless turbulent roads.

We asked for you to clasp these hands,

Touch hearts and souls with your strength.

We ask for your will for all these needs,

Shower them with loving compassion.

I pray, comfort for pain,

Peace, for hurting hearts.

I ask for the thirsty to find refreshment,

I ask for an angel to watch over those.

Uplift family and friends, share your spirit,

With love for your earth children . . .

Psalm 88:2

Philippians 4:6

81

When the wind blows

When the wind blows

Till it knocks me down

Shelter in your arms

Is found

The Rains may pour

They'll take my home

But with you

I'm not alone

My health may fall

I may turn frail

But with you

I cannot fail

My faith is the only key

You have promised paradise to me

No more death, sickness, or strife

I'll look forward to that new life

John 14: 3

The Old Oak

On the ground you lay,

Broken weathered worn,

Like a carcass,

Oh, I'll miss your comfort,

As I walk this path.

Your cool embrace from the sun,

That beat so intense

Your limbs that swayed with the breeze,

Like a dancing the ballet

I will no longer hear your whispers,

When the winds

Blows you to and fro

My beautiful White Oak, Gone . . . .

Isaiah 1:29 & 30

Heaven's Sea

Every morning it's a trip to the Sea.

To watch the ships as they flee.

Oh Bessie can't you see,

He's never coming back to thee.

In the storm his bow did rip.

That's when he made his last trip.

Her mind just won't let it be.

It's his face she longs to see.

At the old bench is where she'll see.

The love she's lost . . .

On Heaven's Sea

Deuteronomy 30:11-13

Where Darkness Grows

Why am I here?

Where darkness grows

Maybe to be a light,

Only He knows!

I feel like a lamb,

Lost in a forest!

What will happen here?

Come closer my dearest . . .

"Let me see your eyes",

Says the wolf.

"Why do you need me this close?", I say!

I'll have you for supper today!!

Isaiah 42:16

Isaiah 42:16

Genesis 50:20

Loosed From Hell

God had taken his chosen home
Satan loosed on earth to roam.

Swung the door once bolted tight
Open to prisoners to take flight

Open now was the gates to hell
Letting demon linger for a spell

Oh they thought it all was fun
Until they found no place to run

Released now in all his fury
Eyes drip with tears all blurry

Pinned, a long one thousand years
Eyes they spit daggers and spears

Scared they dropped to their knees
Sending to heaven worthless please

All who were left heard of this fate
But they waited one day too late . . .

Revelation 20

The Demon

The demon came a took you away

Only your shadow was left to stay

Lost without one single word

To whisper enchantments boldly heard

He locked you in his mega bite grip

As my eyes watched him rip

All that was spoken in dreamers muse

Spreading words and, poems to blues

Might you ever come back again?

Battle the fight and hope to win

This mechanism can't keep you down

The reckoning solution will be found

Matthew 16:23

Rain Down

Healing power rain drops flow

On my broken body blow

Send this illness to the wind

All the way around the bend

Holy Spirit rain your power

Send your anointing on this hour

Father God I need a hand

All through me lovingly send

Thank you father up above

For sending down your pure love

Thank you for raining down on me

I love you just for being Thee

Psalm 72:6

When I First Met You

When I first met you
I had lost all my trust
My heart had harden
It had begun to rust

I had nothing to give
Life had worn me down
I did nothing but live
I built me a wall all around

You took me in your arms
You danced me around
Turned on your charms
All the walls came tumbling down

You ask me to always by your side
You trusted me so much
You had nothing to hide
I learn by your loving guide

That when my heart was oiled
And honed, it came back to life
Thank you for the Patience
I'm happy to be your wife

1 John 4:7-12

The Lord and I Peeled Potatoes

The Lord and I peeled potatoes

It's such a mundane task

I peeled and sang Him praises

While He filled my empty flask

I sang the songs He gave to me

I slowed from all life arrant run

My voice not even middle class

He didn't turn away to run

But as my voice filled the house through

God's Spirit chased away feeling of blue

He knew that I needed that mundane task

To smooth lives heavy day past

Romans 8:1 & 2

Love Struggles

I have been let down
I have been run around
Many claimed to have love
Action is reality you see

The struggle not to love you
Fear you will hurt me too
Will you turn my heart blue?
I don't wish to see it in you

You turn my mind on end
Do things to make me spin
Oh, I do not want you to win
Oh, I do so want you to win

Put my heart at ease
Please don't be a tease
Give me what I need
Where will new love lead?

Psalm 71:1-5

New Love

Walking around with that silly turn up smile
half here, half there, up the road a few mile
Don't think I don't know.
I know . . .
Then the music starts to play on your phone,
playing that love song on the ring tone.

That silly smile turns to a teeth showing grin.
Oh, should new love be a sin!

You take your call in whispered roams.
Till your laugh rings loud, then Dad groans

Don't think I don't know.
I know . . .
Then you come in, set, looking,
a little rejected.

He's tired, and needs to sleep.
This time, you'll have to keep.

Then you start tapping out on your PC.
It seems he really can't sleep.
That silly grin returns then.
With all those charming,
words he sends.
Don't think I don't know.
I know . . .

New love should be a sin!
But I think with this one,
you'll win!

Job 22:13
John 10:27
Psalm 44:21

Spring around the Corner

When your crocus

first sprouts through the snow

this is the time we will know

spring is just around the corner

when we see a robin singing in a tree

we will know

spring is just around the corner

when the short day

start to get a little longer

we will know

spring is just around the corner

when young love comes out

hand in hand, we will know

spring is just around the corner

I am looking forward to, spring around the corner

John 4:14

2 Corinthians 5:17

Nightmare

Waves hit me hard

Swishing ringing in my ear crashing loud

Cold water splashing over and over

My clothes run dripping wet

I set bound to the shore

Ice cold water taste salty on my lips

Scrapes about me burn with each washing wave

Tears mingle with the waves

Running from my wet lashes

I wake, least I think I am,

Yet I am here on my bed dripping cold bound yet not,

Shaken cold but unable to move under the coverlet

Drifting waves roll on dreams to nothing but cold

Finally reality clears in my heavy fogged mind

I wipe at the tears on my cheek,

Look to the half made bed

Shiver at the cold,

I reflect the daylight streaming through sheers

My feet touch the cold floor,

Wishing I had another chance to dream.

Romans 8:38-39

Whispering Prayer

I feel the touch of prayer
Whispering to my soul
I feel it calm the storm
That life brings on so bold

It tells do not fret
Over earthly rendering sand
For here is just a moment
In Christ divinity plan

Take His hand in sorrow
Take His hand to bear
All the trials of life
He will ease your every care

When I do not have the strength
To touch the masters hand
I pray a friend to take my cross
Kneel to take my stand

I will feel the touch of prayer
Whispering in my soul
It will calm the storm
That life brings on so bold

Isaiah 51:11

Wonderful Design

I want to get to know you
Tell me you are here
The snow sprinkled to the ground
To and fro the wind blew

White powder softly danced around
Covering the earth with its blanket
Protecting the seeds
Hid beneath the ground

The wind blew away the chill
With a soft warming breeze
Flower buds peeked from the ground
The Sun rose and warmed the hill

The sun began to lighten the sky
Warmth seeped in the air
Soft music deep in my heart
Started an old tune melody

Playing in my mind
The tune found its way to my lips
One I had learned as a child
Chasing away the time

Leaving all doubts behind
God wrapped me in his love
Showing me His perfect gift
A world of wonderful design

Colossians 1:16

Dancing Dreams

I dreamed I was a ballerina

Standing on pointed toes

Dancing to a melody

Free from human woes

I would twirl around about

I'd jump so very high

I'd touch a white fluffy cloud

Hit the tops of endless sky

When I wake in downed slumber

In a real worlds scene

I long to have another prance

In the land of a dancing dream

Psalm 149:3

His Fields

We think that the seed is just a seed we plant

But we are the seed that God has lent

He put us to work to harvest fields

Bringing in his loving yields

We must work at it every day

To be as loving in his way

To give of our self when the need

Giving and nurturing us his seed

To be more and more like him

To bring in people for him to win

Psalm 126:6

Isaiah 55:10-11

Hot Water

Anger serves no purpose it doesn't satisfy the wounded

It does not resolve the delinquent

It boils up like a festered infection

Running oozing pus, it runs despondent

In a stink causing an antisocial infestation

Initiating all to tread on broken egg shell

It curves a wedge in a work of soul partnering

It is the death of many, a lonely incarcerated state

Soon festers to include no one but an egotistical

Singular resentful state of incongruousness to the lifeless

Psalm 37:8

Proverbs 15:18

Proverbs 10:12

The Cloud of Dark

The clouds of dark fill the room

You wait the impending doom

The fight was started long ago

The ancient of books tells us so

It's the fight for moral men

Only won by God's hand

The strength is gathered by the voice

Of all the saints as they rejoice

So lift your voice in prayer and praise

It will put the demons in a daze

It will give the angels strength

Even raise the sword in length

When God's people call to him

He is always listening in

He will slay the demon of doom

With the joy he's coming soon!!

2 Corinthians 10:3-5

Insecurity

Why do you come around?

get me all stirred up.

I thought I had put you

in your place long ago.

But here you are

trying to blow

my mind.

Making me be umm, well . . .

I don't like you!

Don't like the way

you make me feel!

Truly a demon playing the mind . . .

You have no grip,

take a trip!

Back to where you belong,

HELL!

James 4:7

There He Is

I finally get to meet the voice I chatted with for hours.

My knees about give when I see him come my way,

His suit jacket flapping like a super hero cape!

His tall firm stance about bowled me over

His baritone voice knocked my mind senseless.

I reach out my meager hand for a shake,

He laughed and brought me into a bear hug

One that about took my breath away . . .

Wow what a presence he brought with him

Those deep brown eyes, eye me over top to bottom.

Then says" Sorry I must be off to my station!"

He takes off with the same stamina he walks in with . . .

My mind whirls and I wonder where to go

I back down into a seat to have a set

As I try to shake my mind back in place

Yet I suddenly feel more alone than when I came in.

Psalm 17:15

Acts 6:15

Flying

In my dreams
I spread my arms
I take off to the sky
watch all that is below
pass by . . .

I am free just like an eagle
going to and fro I sore
No care to this life
no pain, no regrets.

Just flying high,
Above the trees,
above the cities
All look and marvel
that I can fly
way up in the sky.

I knew I could do this,
For so long!
But the weights,
they held me back.
The fact that
humans aren't
suppose to do this.

The fact that,
someone would think
me stupid if I tried.

But now I'm here,
I am so almost free.
I love just being,
me . . . .

Isaiah 40:31

Life for Eternity

I walked along, here on earth
My fate was sealed at my birth
To give my life for my brother
For God's son there was no other

This fate heavy bore me down
I kneeled by a rock I found
Father in Heaven, Please release
Will you make it all to cease

But He bequeathed it up to me
Turned his back for all to see
I knew the angels were at my call
My love for you, wouldn't let me fall

The whip slashed my trembling skin
The thought of you in your sin
For your evil there was a debt
One that had to be paid yet

I knew the pain would be much more
For you my flesh would be tore
They made it public for all to see
As they nailed me to the tree

The nails pierced my hands and feet
My heart thundered with the beat
The pain of love that broke my heart
For me it was the hardest part

But through my death, life for man
To heaven to take you by the hand
You my love could come to me
To now live for eternity.

John 3:16

No Greater Love

You make me dream
Of heavenly things
Praising you with
Abandoned themes

You pick me up
Beyond my own
Brimming my empty cup
To a place at your throne

I don't deserve
What you layout
This reserve
You make me shout

The tears they come
Like falling rain
I think what was won
With your blood stain

Your love abound
From above
They'll be found
No greater love

John 15:13

CHAPTER 4

In The Way

It's been too lone a travel

Without any star

Let the gleams

Whisper your name

Let the shutters open

I'll sing you a song

Chirping heavenly rain

Whimpering dripping pain

I must have been blinded

By a demon within

Cracked through to the brain

To let go your hand, insane

I never fell out of love

The fire took you away

Please take my hand

As me got in my way

Psalm 73:23

Tempting Walk

I try to deny this feeling inside

I would prefer it to walk away

It tags along like a kitten gave milk

Meowing with melancholy sad eyes

It tears my being, strips my good sense

Persuades like that hidden chocolate

Like the tree in the garden it radiates

Come, have of this fruit it will be good

I walk, my head is turned

Like the wife of Sodom

I feel I am a pillow of salt piled high

Dust in the wind lost without you

The clouds gather the sun hides

My dreamers mind sweeps to possible

Yet I resign myself to the drone

Not to act on the drama

1 Corinthians 10:13

The Unicorn

This is quite a mystical creature

many tales I hear.

What is the real reason?

Could it be out of season?

You just don't see the unicorns here!

Some say it's a bad Bible translation.

It really is quite a bad situation.

But the unicorn face you won't see.

For a unique creature is he.

Was it he missed the boat?

While playing tag by the sea?

Is he really a goat?

With a missing horn, is he?

Can the unicorn only be seen by those with?

Exceptional virtue and honesty?

Some of the tales say this is true.

Would I be able to see him?

Is he a good omen that comes?

to humans only on important missions?

All these tales makes me wishing

I could see this beautiful creature!

A folklore tells how in a virgin lap

A unicorn once lay to take a nap

What a treasure to tell,

It would be a wonderful tale.

If a unicorn came to your lap to nap!

Well this is the end of my unicorn legend.

Don't bother to look!

If you want to see such mythical creature

you must look in a fairy tale book . . .

Or the Bible.

Numbers 23:22

Job 39:9-10

Psalm 29:6; 92:10

The King James Version reads Unicorn in the Bible

The Fallen Empire

The empire was a fun place to be

Loud and fun with music abound

The lyrics flowed like honey

The friendship and acquaintances

Laughed, cried and played in harmony

Each adoring the others, differences and all

With understanding, guided by respect

They all blossomed and grew into a banquet

Blooming as no others around the world

One day a heady breeze of ego blew in

It wrapped its evil plot and plans to destroy splendor

Disrupting the beauty all hearts enjoyed

Soon the blossoms lost their luster

The petals fell one by one in melancholy dance

Leaving the bare stems where once beauty reigned

Isaiah 14:12-15

God's Son

They threw you in a deep dungeon,

Waiting for your death deliberation

They brought you before the crowds

To negotiation your deathly fate

Beat him until the blood comes through

Nail him to a cross until death

Break his legs that he won't last

On a cross you took your last breath

The earth shook in shear distress

The temple curtain was tore

The sky went complete dark

Lightening flashed at the evil deed

Because men had killed God's Son!

Matthew 27

Hebrews 6:6

A Walk to Paradise

My mind thinks
I can get through this
My father has sent me
They lash out and grab me
Intent on the torch ahead
I am weak from prayer
But high in the spirit
They throw me in a hole
Dark and bleak
I hear moaning
I bow my head
Praying for the
One making this sound
There is no hope here
They are all the damned
There really is no trial
They should just
Nail us to the tree
They call for me
It's been awhile I can't
Tell how long it's been
There is no light
Or darkness here
Just the coldness of fate
I stand before this ruler
He knows he should let me go
But he washes his hands
To send me to another
I have become the entertainment
The people shout crucify him
I know my fate
They beat me until my flesh is raw
Blood pours from the wounds

They take my clothes
Casting lots to see who owns
The king they mock
A king he shall be
They push down on my head
A crown of thorns
It cuts into my flesh
The blood runs like water
Down my face
They place the cross now
On my shoulder
I stagger at its weight
I drag it down the lane
This is my fate
I can walk no more
But they prod me on
Someone steps up to
Carry the burden
I don't have to go alone
They stop to nail
My hands and feet
I cry out in the pain
A drink now they offer me
Vinegar is what I taste
They puncture my side
The last of my blood
Runs down the tree
A man on my side
Hollers out remember me
Today you will be in
Paradise with me
I cry out it is finished!
He did this for you and me.

John 19:17-37

Jesus Asks "Why?"

Why are they doing this to me?

What have I done?

I taught them with virtue

I taught them with love

Why are they doing this to me?

Didn't I turn their water into wine?

Didn't I feed them?

That all would dine

Why are they doing this to me?

Was this all in vain?

My Sweat turns to Blood

Because of the Pain

Luke 22:43-46

Risen Savior

To the tomb the Mary's went that day

The tears that flowed along the way

To wrap their love with dried herb

Remembering His loving word

When they reached the garden tomb

It was a very different room

The light of angels met them there

Told them to have not fear

He you seek, whom you laid to rest

He has risen! He's endured the test

They went, telling those along the way

Some didn't believe what they had to say

Then they remembered lessons He taught

With the salvation message He had brought

That He must die for human sin

But in three days He'd rise again

Matthew 28

Luke 24

The Quest of a Bunny

I chase you down

To take you out

I don't like anything

You are about

You Fly around

Like it's your house

Almost just as bad

as a mouse!

I use my swifter

to catch you

Soon you will be history

It's no mystery

You have a plot

To join with others

multiply you must not!

Even though you're named bunny

you are not to cuddle honey!

So armed as I am

With work to do

I am coming after you!!

Psalm 35:5

119

PC Blues

I cower in my rocker curled up like a ball,

Grasp in my clutches my favorite stuff doll

I push him tight pressed to my face

This is my favorite security place

The fur on my bear snuggled at my cheek

I resist the thumb sucking, it's for the meek

I start swaying the rocker going to and fro

To lose my computer was such a big blow

1 Corinthians 3:15

Angel Fish

They swim around in beautiful grander

With fins that fly like Heavens sender

Golden wings, kissing lips

Dancing around twisting their hips

Sprinkle of cuisine eye their fancier

To the top like a refined dancer

Oh, the elegance as they flow

Always meddling and on the go

If you take them in your home

In your heart they will roam

With a flight of whimsical charade

All your work will soon fade

Isaiah 26:3

Love is Born

Behold sun dancing slowly across sky meeting stars

The wind whistles a sonnet for lovers

Clouds gather at the far side to watch

Swinging their feet in beat, setting on Milky Way

The meeting is blinding rays arms clasping entwined

The coming together so explosive, a new world is born

The sparks fly blowing tiny stars into existence,

Spreading across the mass darkness dispersing light

The cello plays her melancholy tune with vigor

Joy spreads far a birth, Heaven and Earth rejoice

Love is born in all Heavens and forever

God sets back in his Heavenly throne,

Sighs at His handy work with a smile

Genesis 1:13-18

Sauntering Lone

The hills of life seem lonely

Like the ocean endless on shore

Reflecting the sauntering moon light

The light companionship for the lone

With heart that beats in a gentle soul

The song relaxing into the space softly

Shadows turn away from the lone door

The breeze whispers a rainbow

But no where can I find my dream

I am lost like the beacon in a cloud

The kiss of yesterday haunts mortality

Yet dawn winds whisper a new love

Isaiah 51:2

Kissing the Dew

The rain drop danced through the meadow

Skipped to the bubbling shallow creek

Was lost in the raging stormy gray flood

Thrust to the over flowing river to meet

Pushed forward in the throng of the crowd

Caught in the entanglements mass snare

Rushed to the joining of lumped gathering

Stripped of his distinction to thread bare

Void in this evil vast worthless expanse

Yet observing gray clouds wondering why

Suddenly thrust in a slick black nothing

Yearning for a grassy meadow and blue sky

Now knowing this is the end of his journey

As in a mist he is carried on high . . .

A pure rain drop lost to black oil

Brings me a heart to rending sigh

Psalm 72:6

Isaiah 53

Lonely

It drops like molasses from a tree

Running down into my soul

Dark as night with no light

Drip, drip, drip

It veils my heart without

Voice, void of sound

Rambling unsettled mind

Drip, drip, drip

Filling this melancholy bucket

With a slow steady stream

Sweet as apple vinegar

Drip, drip, drip

John 14:18

Gentle Rain

Gentle rain you fill me my cup

You're the one to bring me up

Don't need any sunshine shining down

It's you I want around

I am the garden, you quench my thirst

You take care of me at my worst

Gentle rain I need your love

Coming down straight from above

When I hear the thunder clap

It makes me happy in your lap

Because I know you'll soon be with me

It's only you I long to see

Psalm 72:6

Angel Dance

I hear the sound

As their feet hit the floor

I hear the clap

As the lightning roar

There is an old story

From long ago

The thunder happens

When Angels tap their toe

Oh what a ruckus

The Angels make as they prance

I look up to the heaven

Hoping to see angels dance

But the thunder clapped

And spoiled my fun

It was so loud

I took off to run

Revelation 19:17

Luke 2:7-15

Love Whispers

Love walks in starry night and morning mist

Less it is the first light that sees the sky

Or the last to drop in twilight shining eye

Holding tight yet the need to whisper bye

But dreams go with a ship of togetherness

Ever in the silent ripping storm of weather

Eyes closed in restful slumber swaying in tune

The love never leaves it lives in each whisper

Dancing on the melody of enchanted time

Singing a song of meeting you on heavens shore

While riding the beams in tomorrow's chamber

A enlighten thoughtful vision as ever walked

1 Kings 19:11 & 12

The Ark

They laughed as Noah built the Ark
Of his truth they wouldn't hark
He told them they wouldn't float
To heed the call get in the boat!

But they thought he was insane
Thought his words all in vain
They laughed when the rain first came
And said on land they would remain

But as the water became deep
Tears in their eyes began to seep
When in their homes the water crept
They knew it would grow in depth!

At the Ark they began to knock
God is the one who bolted the lock!
The waters rose to lift the boat
All inside began to float . . .

Genesis 6 and 7

Sleeping Melody

I wake to the morning of dreams

Rise to dance on toes in loves step

Swaying I sing an exhaling song

Does anyone listen to this melody?

Lest it be lost to the winds

I send my voice on Heavens wings

She sighs in her breezy breath

Trees take up an ocean sway

Wind ruffles the grass singing

I lay my head in its softness

The lullaby lulls me to sleep

Like a babe in the cradle

Psalm 40:3

In Another Day

Like a movie star in a leading role
I write a part
Of lovers from far off countries
Of mind not heart

Some take it so serious
Do not take it that way
It a living
In another day

I can write of dragons
Are they real
Have you ever seen?
a one hundred foot chameleon?

Have you been to a world?
with two or more moons
with both of them setting
by the high noon

I can write of space
the man in the moon
puckering his lips
to whistle a tune!

Psalm 102:18

131

Life's Chapters

Drip, Drip, Drip
The ceiling rains with memory
A pot catches the water
The dew on my cheek
Flows like a creek

The ghost of child laughter
A voice macho and strong

A cane clatters to the floor
I stoop to pick it up
Awake now from my dream
An empty house
Cold, damp and old

The stories of another time
Wrapped in its binder
I read the last chapter
In this Land of Oz

Lock the door, close the book
To a ghost of child laughter
A voice macho and strong
Drip, Drip, Drip . . .

Psalm 37:25

The Struggle

I hear you
I don't want to
I would rather play
You touch me
You call softly
I brush your hand away
You stand back
I go my way
Rain flows from Heaven
You watch
I turn away
Distances grows
Your hand reaches
I feel your fingertips
They cling to hope
Beckoning me to your arms
I hear the music
The laughter, it calls
I turn away again
Not wanting to see
Pained eyes
I walk away
Is that a sob?
Is it from you?
No it must be my soul.
I walk away . . .

Judges 10:16
Proverbs 27:8
Jeremiah 2:20

Waiting For Your Kiss

Lips quiver as they await your touch
Whispers of breath touch my cheek
Heat from your nearness sieves in
Heart races to win in completion

Anticipation reads on my dewy skin
The pages flip through my mind
Read like a popular love novel
The melody raises the tempo

Floating on the clouds of endless sky
Sprinkled with the rays of sunshine
Prisms dance the steps expectancy
It's ominous how you manipulate

Screen the life from me moaning
Lustrous feasts the mind mounting
Sprouts shoot to through the ground
Caressing the daylight with green

Then your lips finally touch mine
I melt running like honey in a puddle
Fire shoots to the exploding sky
I loose myself in the pliable dream

Songs of Solomon 1:2

Knowing You Care

Knowing you care
You are always there

Touching our life
Through the sorrow and strife
A prayer breathe away to
Help with the day

I can feel joy
Through each girl and boy
The flowers that bloom
While pushing the broom

Sunshine or rain
Comfort or pain
Life's an easier ride
With You by my side

Like the sea coming in
You care if I win
We walk down this road
Surrendering you the load

Knowing you care
You are always there

Hebrews 13:5

Tears, a Language

Tears are the flow of emotion

when the heart is full

tears are joy

tears are sorrow

tears, when we are speechless

tears a language

God understands

tears are a breaking

of spirit

a silent call

for God to help

tears are healing

tears a language

God understands

Psalm 56:8

Ask His Son

God sends down his hand
On wings of gentle angel band

He will take you to his home
No more to wonder or roam

When this life on earth is done
If you have this but ask his Son

Believe that he died for you
Ask him if you can come too

Then he'll give your heart a lift
This is His life, a precious gift

Acts 16:31

Washed Ashore

The sea washed you into my caring arms

I wrap you in my purple cloak

Half dead you look to my arms in trust

Ones you noted encouragingly apt

On my furry bed I lay you down

Watching slumber color recover your soul

You know not the power you stole within me

I discern you stole much more and wept

Rains took me to slumbers dream

Lost in ocean tide wave by wave

Where visions endure to weep

Transfixed by the morning mist

Prisms at play like angels dance

Across the white lily exotic face

My wish to stay in this safe haven

Yet my restless soul stirs deep

2 Samuel 15:6

A Mother's Prayer

Dear Lord,

Could you spare some Guardian Angels?

to give me peace of mind,

As my children wonder from me,

and stretch the ties that bind.

You have heavenly Legions, Father.

Could you send me just a few?

to guide my eager young stars.

As I give them Lord to you.

Oh, thank you, thank you Father and,

Oh my glad heart sings,

I'm certain that just now,

I heard the swish of passing wings . . .

My sister wrote this Poem before she died April 29, 1984.

She left 7 children.

This was found by her bedside

by Janet Tackett RIP

1 Corinthians 6:3

Remembering You

As the spring brings
the flower of new hope
You would give in
Let go of the rope

The pain that you bore
Much too long
You would leave now
For an angel song

We so miss
Your fun smile
Your giving nature
You'd walk a mile

You left us a legacy
One to fill
One to challenge
Our very will

You loved the Lord
With a bold shout
You told us
What he was all about

Now you walk
While holding his hand
One day we will join you
Where angels stand

John 11:25-26
In remembrance of loved ones gone on

Ring the Bells

Ring the bells of church so true
Wash away my thoughts of blue
Sing a song the spirit to lift
Is a Holy kind of gift?

Ring the bells of church so true
Tell me a story of Christ or two
I know if I concentrate on Him
In the end a new life I'll win

Ring the bells of church so true
I'll kneel and pray till your will I do
In this land of trouble and strife
You give me hope to have new life

Ring the bells of church so true
Help others to hear of you
Help them understand your why
To forget about this earth of lies

Psalm 43:3

Matthew 5:14

CHAPTER 5

Bubbling Joy

It's bubbling in my soul

Oh the joy it can't be told

Jesus gave his love to me

I have to share for all to see

It overwhelms me at times

Helps me write all my rhymes

He is my precious friend

Just for me, God has sent

It's because he loves me so

To easy life burdens of woe

Oh the joy it makes me prance

Here I go I have to dance!

Isaiah 61:3

Birthing Spring

Waiting beneath the soil

For the first heat from Suns warm touch

Inching forward in the hope of spring heat

Tales flourish shared by elders' seed

The green excited newness

Dancing to bring it's budding

Waiting for warmth to embrace

Imparting the cold of yesteryear

Chasing away the gray clouds

With a kiss to new loves ground

Bringing color to a sleeping world around

2 Peter 3:18

The Story of My Love

You are the story of my love

You are the dreams I wander by day

The dreams I slumber by night

You are the smiles

That catches my unaware lips

The words to my poems

The song in my heart

You are the longing

I knew not I had

You are my fantasy

My vision of reality

You are the story of my love

Psalm 42:1

I Can Hear

But I have other things

I wish I could most hear when artist sing

I miss this the most

I miss the words as others talk

I am glad I have learned to text

but not everyone does yet

there are obstacles to overcome

everyone has some . . .

You see I can't hear a lot of sound

Yes, I am almost deaf

But Please don't

ignore me

Your heart I can hear

I can hear . . .

Proverbs 8:5-6

Heart's Path

The broken rhinestone sets on the counter
A reminder of dreams left unfilled
A beautiful gem left with scars
Beautiful yet with its uneven parts

The heart is an amazing thing
It can reroute its vital life giving blood
Giving you more time on earth
Opening new passages

Still parts would be dead
Is it not what was intended?
We change our destination by choice
Like a monopoly being played out?

Watch and protect
Pray and choose wise
For you can't detect
What in your life lies?

Ask the Lord
To give you a hand
Do what's accord
For him to stand

Psalm 22:26
Proverbs 15:13

A Supernatural Book

This book I read is so fair.

I'm always reading something different there!

Sometimes I'm in a rough Sea. (Matt 8:23)

Sometimes of fire is what the story will be! (Dan 3:19)

There are impossible battles. (Josh 6)

There are men with lots of cattle! (Gen 13)

There is a wedding to beat all.

Bigger than any dancing Ball! (John 2)

A Giant over nine feet tall! (1 Sam: 17)

A tower that is forced to fall! (Gen 11:4)

There are animals two of every kind. (Gen 6 19)

Wisdom to break chains that bind! (Isaiah 61:1)

A talking donkey! (Numbers 22)

Man swallowed by a whale! (Dan 3:25)

Food falling from Heaven, like hail! (Exodus 16:14)

Water is turned to wine. (John 2:9)

Fish abundant, that all can dine! (Mark 6:30)

What's this supernatural book I read?

It's the B-I-B-L-E.

Psalms 119:11

Broken Paths

You refresh my thirsty soul
You bring me up from my despair
Sow joyful tears to my hardened heart
All the while whispering I care

This feeling, like no other
You bring me to your light
I don't know how I understand
But this feeling is simply right

Jesus a name so wonderful
Left heaven for my eternal life
Kisses my brow in sorrow
As I tarry through earthly strife

I may turn my back
Forget you for a little while
When I turn to face you
You meet me with a smile

Gentle arms embrace
This weathered earthly child
Bring me back to your hold
So tender merciful and mild

Acts 3:19

The Journey

She rode like an attachment to the stallion
Pressing hard with the embedded knees

Hair waving in the breeze
Like the flag of the kingdom

The awesome creature gallops
Thrusting forward at her command

The thrash of the leather
Pinches his muscled side

With the urgent influence from the rider
Like a life balanced in the chased

The journey ahead travels on
A terrain hard, rough and long

The path is slim and sparingly traveled
In the eyes sight, there shows a garden

Walls sparkle of polished Jasper
Streets so pure gold they shine clear

A gate of pearl reflecting light
A just reward for the extensive journey

A shining light that beams
The Kings smiles

Psalm 18:30

You've Got Mail

A heartsick Boy,
A lonely girl

Meet in a space,
Where neither can touch

But with words,
Express what they need

From something worn
A flower is born

The secrets they bare
The life cruelties they share

They touch with the words,
They tap out on keys

It opens a door,
Like a summer breeze

For a companionship,
Neither has possessed.

They only dreamed to see each other
Share this love one for another!

Psalm 88:18
Songs of Solomon 5:16

Forever My Love

As time goes on I still see the girl
That stepped down the petal aisle
The twinkle in her sky blue eyes
That still makes my heart fly

You made my heart do a spin
I knew long ago we would win
I don't see faded hair
Your beautiful life I share

I feel the connection before we touch
I feel when you walk into the room
You have become a part of me
The part that opens in bloom

It happened the day I seen your smile
As it danced across the sun
I could look into your eyes a mile
As they enlighten with fun

Here we reach the golden years
I know why it is thus called
Because I know I'll dance with you
Forever in Heavenly halls

Jeremiah 31:3

Wind Whispers

I love you my child
I close my eyes
accepting the embrace
the touch brings a tear

The content welcome
like a spring bubbling from
a lost fountain in the desert
a welcome refreshment to quench

a soul of thirst
Making for a light heart
in a torrent of earthly woe
Take me with thee I plea

I love you my Lord
"Every step, I am by your side
Live for me . . ."
I step to walk away

looking back not seeing him
Then I hear the wind blow
with a gentle whisper,
"I'm right here . . ."

John 15:15
Proverbs 18:24

I Close My Eyes to Dream

I close my eyes to dream

Dream of another land

Land that shines moisten drops

Drops not made of tears

Tears that fall like rain

Rain that shines like gold

Gold that brings the light

Light will bring my tears to close

I close my eyes to dream

2 Corinthians 4:18

Shaking Rugs in the Rain
(A Mother's Day Story)

I didn't want to go to church today.

You see they line all the mothers up front to give us a flower,

I don't mind flowers, I actually love them!

But then they want you to say a little something.

The first lady tells how she praises God all her children are doing God's work!

The next lady tells how she was raised in Africa because her family was missionaries.

Praise the Lord! And so it goes on.

I am praising the Lord here today.

I think of the struggles our family has had!

I am just happy we made through!

I think I'll just stay here today and shake my rugs.

It is raining hard!

The dirt joins with the rain and falls to the ground.

My rugs are getting clean; they will look nice on my floor.

I'm sure I am not the only one that feels like shaking rugs today.

I'm pretty sure David's Mom didn't always feel like going to church on Mother's Day.

But God said, He was a man after his own Heart.

Sam, His Mom would have loved that flower!

The job He done, there at the end, Wow!

So, I'll just Stay home and shake my dirty Rugs.

I'll watch as the dirt joins with the rain drops.

It will settle in my flower garden in the front.

I'll go get some flowers to plant in it this week.

The dirt will feed them, and they will grow!

I will look back at this rainy day with a smile.

I'll remember the day I stayed at home to shake my rugs in the rain.

I'll rejoice in the beautiful flowers in my garden,

I'll think of the dust from my rugs,

The ones I stayed home to shake in rain.

Psalm 113:9

Did You Hear That

Did I say that aloud?
For no one to hear
Shush don't tell
Insanity I fear

I walk to my plants
I'll give them a drink
Tell me my mind
What do you think?

What should we do?
What must be done?
Walking through my mind
I want to have fun

Did you hear that?
My flower so dear
I'm talking to you
I know you can hear

Was that a wink I seen?
From the corner of my eye
I must take time to think
I'm talking out loud,

If I am caught
Being this bold
It will turn my face pink

Deuteronomy 5:24

Windowsill

Let the light shine in my windowsill

That you may see, if be your will

That you might see a lighted sign

Whisper hope to me in time

I'll try best to gain your heart

If life you'll offer me a part

Our love is not a fantasy

I give my heart all to thee

I'll create for you a loving throne

I'll make you king of all I own

Hand in hand I'll dotingly share

All my life with you to bear . . .

Psalm 118:27

Prism Bird

Whispering mist sprays morning dawn

crystal seas join in with song

my mind drifts the gentle sea

the love that is you and me

the tree top sway with the beat

my heart time they keep

in percussion I drift to you

a song as deep royal blue

hush now don't say a word

send it with a prism bird

wings flutter in dawn light

everything will be alright

2 Peter 1:19

With God's Love

On this earth I have not wealth

I have not even perfect health

But I have a work to do

Bring God's Love to offer you

I may not have the perfect words

But perfect words are misunderstood

I am here for now to stay

To bring some help in my own way

It won't scream or be bold

But His story must be told

In gentle spirit you can see

With God's love,

all you can be . . . .

2 Timothy 1:6-9

Butterfly Kisses

Touch of butterfly kisses

Feathering across my skin

Loves warm body

Close to mine

Pulled into the warm embrace

Rocked to slumber

Enduring songs tickling my ear

Scents of roses close

Snuggled tight in dream slumber

Fields of daisy sway by the winds breath

Chariots of clouds play close by

Soft dream, Keep me here

Ecclesiastes 3:1

Flight of the Butterfly

Dancing through the air

with the lightest of breeze

Fluttering around sprinkling their power

All the while landing on every flower

A soft kiss of encouragement to grow

Is all in the touch they magically bestow

Off they are to a faraway land

On the paths of ocean sands

Bringing a smile with their enchanting beauty

Joining together in flight like it's their duty . . .

Lifting our spirit with an enchanting glory

Inspiring us with their alluring story

Isaiah 52:7

The Meeting

The dark of his eyes,
are like pools that reflect the moon.
I feel warmth that floods my very being.
He looks my way;

I see my reflection in those eyes
The instant attraction is as primitive
As the first meeting of man and women,
At the very introduction from God!

Her eyes are as blue as the sky
at high noon on a clear day
I can't explain this feeling
But it is much like wrestling a bull

and he has knocked the wind out of me . . .
My breath is caught in my chest
constricting the vital life
I need to survive . . .

Our coming together was appointed before we were.
We could not stop it if we wanted.
Our lips have been set in stone.
No words can be formed.

A spell so strong, there is no cure, No remedy . . .
But to meet this, my destined Love!!

Songs of Solomon 8:5-7

Curb Side Shopping

Curb side shopping,
Oh what fun for the artist in me!

Curb side shopping
you can go on a spree!
Because you fill up your auto,
all for free!

I have a beautiful, coffee table.
Someone just wasn't able,
to see the vision of what it could be!

Just a little paint!
A treasure now for all to see!!
Curb side shopping doesn't bother me!

For someone's thrown out!
Mixes my mind about,
what a gem of a treasure,
will come next to see!

I know you all will wish
you could go with me.
when you see
what fills my house?
With wonderful finds

I tell you there were no lines
it's all truly mine
and I didn't spend a dime!!

take my advice
for it is nice.

To share all the treasure stories
with friends and the glories,
of beautiful artifacts for free!

Matthew 13:52

A Poet Day

A poet's heart flutters to wake

Thoughts open castle doors

Wheat stands at attention

As tree limbs clap and wave

Fruit grows round and full

Butterfly flutter and birds sing

Oh to imagine all these things

Can you hear the steps the spider crawls?

Can you hear the fly rub his tentacle claw

The cat lay lazy as the mice dance

Sing to me, voice of Puccini

My mind may wonder where to play

Soft as baby sleeps, loud as a mother weeps

Rhymed as the marching band

All this rambling in my mind

Quite tiring a lot of time

Heavy lashes touch my cheek

Butterfly kisses light to sweep

Closing the door to the wake

It won't take long for me to travel

The dreamland window cracks its shadow

1 Corinthians 3:13

A Peter Pan Heart

My heart soars at your gentle kiss

You bring your head around to whisper in my ear

Soft touching fingers on my hair

A glance of innocence glistens from silver shining eyes

I catching you looking, when you don't think I see

You move my heart, your shadow always on my mind

Stars shoot across the sky as we meet

We walk this world of Neverland to dream

Playing hide and seek between the enchanting stars

Dancing the gentle touch calling to dream

When you are gone I dream your smile, Smell your lily rose

Feel softness of your cheek touching mine

I remember taking your hand, the magic

mystery thundered with lightning flashing

The clouds part as we walk through his path

Letting in the sunshine to smile along our journey

Ephesians 3:19

Where Poems Grow

It's a place I go

Or maybe a time

Where poems grow

The word starts to rhyme

It's a dream of long ago

Where life sends a mellow flow

Dancing on thoughts to no end

Bringing my mind a lasting friend

To release my creative stance

Whipping wind a mind to prance

Dreams are dreams of telepathy

It's a stupendous place to be

Job 32:8

Nature Walk

The bubbling brook rides hugs rocks

A flap of wings as birds flock

The chirping bird gathers seed

Their babies cry the need to feed

The crunch of twigs under step

To clear the mind of past regret

A startled fawn runs away

Hoping you're not here to stay

Breathing deep in the fresh air

Hoping to release a world of care

A calming walk through God's creation

Easing life's expectations

Revelation 5:13

Across The Sky

Do thou hear His earthly cry?

Soon He'll come across the sky

Illuminating wings, saunter by

Calling to some, but not to you,

Do thou wonder why?

Remember when He called your heart?

For you to get on board the ark

But you stayed to play in the rain

Left out of the wash you have a stain

He can't hear your calling voice

It's covered by the ones who rejoice

Isaiah 55:6

Genesis 6:3

If These Walls Talked

When these walls talked, what did they say?

One of these will be president some day?

Will Bobby Jones make the mark?

Why Susan Ann is smart as a lark!

When these walls talked they didn't say

One day they will take prayer away!

They didn't talk of evolution,

But how to solve a math solution . . .

When these walls talked they didn't say

will these kids be safe today?

The worst would be he'd pull her hair

it just a fun and simple dare.

If these walls talked, they would say

come back to a simpler day.

Psalm 78:31-34

Isaiah 44:22

Isaiah 55:7

We've Danced

I write, 'I love you' in the sand

The only time I let go of your hand

The stars shine bright in your pale eyes

It's funny how fast time flies

Just yesterday, you walked a petal trail

That day you set my heart to sail

We didn't even take time to date

There was no reason for us to wait

The moment my eyes looked at you

Like the heavens I simply knew

That you were made for only me

You knew too, I was made for thee

We've danced to this romance of life

Side by side, through happy and strife

Not swayed by wind as it blew

Holding hands as the music flew

Ecclesiastes 3:4

Void of Words

You see in the morning when I wake up.

It's always been part of the makeup.

Run to the paper and pen

write whatever, God does send . . .

It could be a long dramatic scene.

Something cute and short, but just as keen!

But today the words didn't come!

So I'm writing this for fun!

Void of words.

What can I say?

This came on in an unusual way.

Isaiah 55:11

Immortal Hope

The sun always enjoyed the shadows

When the Moon came out to play

Hoping to meet him in another day

She listened from afar to all the songs

Inspired that his heart lovingly used

Longing for the soul,

That sung such in his muse

.

The longing grew to love

When they both learned to communicate

Thinking they could meet to saunter some date

But the distance was so far

Between the night and day

They could not come together

There did not seem away

But the hope was immortal

When the Sun and Moon would both retire

Lounge beside a star to whisper away the hour

Matthew 19:26

Making of a Star

The moon shines on your face

The light in your eyes reflect the stars

You search my face with finger tips

I fold your hand in mine, caress it to my cheek

I close my eyes to warmth, on my face

I wake with my hands clasp under my cheek

The blaze of the full moon reflects in the water its twin

Light ripples splashing to shore,

A fish jumps for its meal

The cannibalism causes me to shiver

Warm sand caress my feet

Soft breeze feels heavenly on my skin

I whisper your name,

Can you hear me?

You break on your morning walk

Meditate on the rising sun

You hear breeze whisper your name

Soft in the voice of love

The sound is like wings on a butterfly

You moan the answering name

It floats on love's breath

The two names collide like two butterflies

Fluttering, dancing, turning playing joyful

They rise to pass the moon in their fluttering unity

Light gleams from their wings

Erupting light flashes, at their joining

A new star is born in heaven

One that will shine for lover's eons to come

1 Corinthians 15:41

CHAPTER 6

The Date

Gathering sea shells
down by the shore

wonder where this will take me
dreaming of more

slipping my hand through
your fingers to twine

Walking to the corner
stand to dine

Kissing the catsup
away from my lips

Blinking my heart
Grows full to rip

Not wanting to leave you
Knowing the evening must end

Back up to heaven
you I must send

Psalm 91:14

Take Time for Love

The sapphire sea shines with crystal sun

The reflection making angels' dance in fun

Mist kisses their heavy wings with enchanted dew

It is told, the dew drops when love is through

When the dew opens, it pours like rain

Causing the earth all kinds of pain

Dance long with the full moon light

Dew drops falling bring clouded fright

Hold tight to loving heartstrings

Until the mind lets loose and sings

Stop to listen to what angel say

Take time for love, with each new day

Ecclesiastes 3:8

If I Were a Bird

If I were a bird
A sparrow I would be
Nipping at a crust of bread
Some one left for me
I would not be so grand
As other birds in the tree

For of my beautiful cousins
Trouble comes their way
Some caught up in a cage
To live throughout their day
I am free to flutter
And go about my way

My home is in the garden
Up in the tall spruce tree
I drink of the morning dew
Watch as God paints a sunrise
All of it for free

Now you know why
I set upon this branch
Singing my heart out with glee
I am looking to the heavens
To the God,
that made me, me

Luke 12:24

Battle Song

I wrote a song

in my sleep last night

All the notes jumped

off the paper, began to fight!

Blocking with bars

and a shield of G cleft

Stabbing with half notes,

whole notes took flight

None would take a rest,

until the lines got up and left!!

Psalm 18:39

Stephen and Persecution

He was such a young man
Full of Christ the Lord Savior

Teaching the gospel
With love and favor

Understanding much for his age
Preaching with a vibrant rage

Leaving his home to roam
It was part the political Nome

Government saw him as a threat
They say his claim inept

Blasphemy is what they say!
Death is the sentence he will pay!

He will die one said intoned
In turn all picked up a stone . . .

Look its heaven opened to me,
It's Jesus whom I see!

With stones they seized his life
He took it all in strife

They turned a blinded ear
Unable they wouldn't hear

He knelt and asks the Lord
To spare His noble sword

To forgive each these slayers
For the mind is bent to layers

For heaven was his home
Where he bequest to roam

You say this was so long ago
Christians today still suffer so

Persecution is still around
Death for teaching the gospel found

Everyday someone dies
For teaching God's word

Some say are lies . . .
Pray for those who live in fear

To reach those who need to hear.

Acts 6:5

Heaven's Place

I hear Your footsteps walking

I feel the dirt beneath my feet

I see You're shining light approaching

I'm unworthy Your Holiness to see

I feel Your spirit touching

Let me sing to hear Your voice

Washing me to be free

From all that haunts in me

Heal my body and spirit

I hold my head up in praise

You touch this mundane soul

Lifting me to Heavens Place

Ephesians 1:3

Sandy's run

Sandy was an avid runner

she ran up her lane like thunder

Sandy's other name was Pied Piper

the neighborhood animals ran beside her

They all would parade down her lane

even Sometimes during bouts of rain

Bats, cats, dogs and pigs

all doing the run a ma jigs

If you want to have some fun

watch for Sandy's next run!

Ecclesiastes 9:11

The Writer's Muse

It is a cold June Morning

I shiver as I open the door

My kitten wraps around my ankle

As I feed her Hunger

The mystery of writing whirls in my mind

Waiting for the chance to dance in print

Endless thoughts and dreams

A gift from God in Heaven

I spread my hands to touch the keys

My intimate world

Where I go to bring fruition

To such a rambling of my mind

The keys reach out wrapping their hugs

The screen illuminates of a love

Where enchanting dreams form

Where anything can happen

2 Corinthians 3:3

The Bride

She dons her crown of pure white
Slips on her shoes a little tight

Steps up to the antique mirror
In the back a mother's tear

In the frame the formal beauty
Preacher marks his page with duty

A little smile to hide the fear
For the unknown a flash of tear

Then her mind, glimpses her love
A soft prayer sent to above

A loving peace a wedding gift
Sent for all the doubts to lift

Then she steps into the isle
At the end a loving smile

With his love he is sending
A promise, happy ever after ending

Revelation 21:2-3

I'm With You

My baby said he'd buy me a Jaguar

I'll love driving that fancy car

I'm gonna stop by the Goodwill

It will be fun drivin' to a yard sale

Can't pass those flea markets

I'll have stares when I park it

Can't wait to fly high

You'll see me pass by

Driving my Jaguar

Like I'm some squire

I'll accelerate that V twin

With you beside me I win

No matter what we do

I'm in heaven with you

Proverbs 23:5

White Drawn Sword and Silver Shield

They watch on seats that are made of cloud

Ready should the master allow?

To come and fight for our quest

They watch us and never rest

They sigh when we don't pass the test

They only want what's for our best

With white drawn sword and silver shield

They will make any demon yield

They want to hear our redemption story

When we tell it up in glory

When we've won an ongoing battle

They shout so, it makes heaven rattle

Know that even when you feel alone

They are watching to help you atone

If you feel a rush of wind

It might be an Angel wing

Psalm 91:11

Matthew 4:6

Luke 4:10

Yours

I will dance with you till morning light

We will dance away the night

I will look into your eyes so kind

I'll see the stars that reflect from mine

We will walk where your garden grows

Whispering secrets only God knows

I will tell you of my love so true

You will embrace me, say you love me too

The last star fades to end the night

The sky turns to dawns first light

You will ask to be my only one

I'll be yours until life on earth is done

Ezekiel 16:8

Mirror, Mirror on the Wall

Mirror, Mirror
On the wall
Who's the fairest of them all?
Only God's Grace
Only By God's Grace

See these bright and shiny eyes
They reflect God's light on high
Like the stars set in the skies
And the birds that fly on by
Only God's grace
Only By God's Grace

He's in the Spirit of Me and you
If you look you'll see Him Too
He binds us with his agape Love
Coming down from above
Only God's Grace
Only By God's Grace

Now we see but through a mirror
Only by his words we hear
But when we are over there
We will see as crystal clear

Only God's Grace
Only By God's Grace

1 Corinthians 13:12
Ephesians 2:5

Another Fairytale

Fairy tales where dreams come true
It is where I think of you
Won't you be my fairytale?
This fantasy life we'll share
We will both wear beauty there

You will have all your wants
I won't play my silly stunts
With diamond in your long hair
No troubles will we have to bear
Everything will be taken care of there

You will be the only lover in my sight
In my arms I'll hold you tight
Everything will be alright
In this fairytale we won't fight
You'll be there when I turn out the light

Not just a dream I have at night
Won't you be my fairytale?
We can live happily ever after there
You won't be just in my dream
We will be a forever team

John 14:2-3

To The Market

To the market we will go while I hold your hand

the grapes so sweet the books are grand

the antiques take you to another time

where candies a penny and soda a dime

Elvis, his ballads turned rock and roll

each vender a different tale as we stroll

turning a pot hoping there a worthy name

as I play this adventurous hunting game

enjoying the weather while hoping for treasure

oh what a pleasure beyond the hearts measure

while we saunter on hand in hand

to every eccentric sellers stand

Proverbs 21:20

True Love

Awe to have cherished love

the angels above

would flap their wings

their heart would sing

Dancing on every cloud

in arms so proud

numbered all sevens

your love from the heavens

See this one's for you

please don't be blue

you'll get your love

and it'll be true

Galatians 5:22

A Father's Heart

I watched as you took your first step.

You let go of my finger.

I watched as you went to school that first day.

You looked so bold

as you went your way.

I watched as you went on that first date.

My heart ran cold,

when he kissed you.

I walked with you down that isle

the preacher said, "who gives her?"

My heart was weak

I turn around to my seat.

I thought how I'll miss you . . .

Revelation 21:9-10

The Lost

I cry for the innocence lost

The times I seen you pray in praising

He who was once your Lord

You're not dead, not in the human sense

His spirit moans for your touch

Gone in the worst way, lost!

Caught up in this life

I wish I could do something

Tell Him to bring you back

But, I know I can't reach you

Only the Love of Christ

can touch a heart . . .

John 6:44

Sweet Love

Sweet love, oh my true love

Let me hold you close to my heart

Heavens here, oh right here

Held in my arms tangled warm

Oh sing to me, with angel songs

Breathing warm breath to mine

Dreamy eyes, loving eyes

Skin smooth as the summer dew

Kissing lips, soft warm lips

Openly, I cannot resist

Slowly move closer yet

All forgot but your touch

Sweet love, oh my true love

Let me hold you close to my heart

Heavens here, oh right here

Held in my arms tangled warm

Genesis 29:18

At The End of the Aisle

I remember the day
I walked down the aisle
you were there waiting
for me at the end.
It was the start of a life together.

Through the years
we have been there one for the other
in pain, in joy
a new home
Children came and went.

We had times of nothing
times of abundance.
No matter what,
I knew I had you
And you had me.
At the end of the aisle,
you wait for me.
In your Blue satin bed
I must say goodbye
For now my love . . .
But someday
I'll come to you. You'll be waiting.
At the end of Heaven's aisle
A smile on your face.
You'll tell me,

Welcome my Love
You have won,
The race . . .

Daniel 12:12 & 13

Poet Dreaming

I'm swept away in your story
With my cup I trip around
You take me to a far off land
Where melancholy abounds

My toast has grown cold
Let me step into your tale
Tales to a dragon land bold
I close my eyes for us to sail

I have entered into your lair
A poets maze to dreams
The words we both hold dear
Only a kindred spirit beams

Lost in this worlds encampment
Where only happy endings live
Like the dreamers to enchantment
Where sky only has blue to give

This is how I want to feel
I may never go back home
I may never click my heel
I'll live in your tale to roam . . .

Acts 17:28

Through Eternities End

Failed relationships hurt me
I was at my wits end
But Jesus was waiting
to heal all my sin

He whispered He loved me
a love I would never find
from any moral mankind
with His arms open wide

A love that had no limit
A love that would never bend
A love that would take me
through eternities end

A love unconditional
A love that says
come just as you are
Here I am always a friend

If you let me in your heart
I will never turn and part
I'll wrap you in my arms
keep you from all harm

I will always be there
To hear your every care
Even when you stumble
and walk out on me!

Simply turn right around
and that's where I'll be.

1 John 4:7 & 8
Jeremiah 31:3

The Proposal

You hold me with your look,

That's all that it took.

To sweep me off my feet

You are wonderfully so sweet . . .

A whisper in the air,

Tells me that you care

By your loving touch,

My heart begins to rush.

Now down on one knee,

For everyone to see

You will always be,

The only one for me . . .

1 John 4:10-12

Love Glance

Long auburn hair glistening sunshine rays

Pale eyes kissed with the blue of sky

Stole shared look a lover's dream

Intimate shy virginally unrequited

Grasp with moonstruck reflection

Visions of reaching arms embracing

Oh, dance with me the dance of love

Entwine me in your likened snare

Hold close this enraptured life

That we may soar with eagles

Glistening wings in holy heavens

Married with divine celebration

Esther 2:17

Blooming Love

This hint of a poem

Blooms at my thoughts

Talking for hours

Of nothing bought

New love snuggles

Watching the sun

Watching people

All on the run

Content With fingers

Laced and entwine

Anything together

anything with you is fine

I will be here

Watching the stride

My head on your shoulder

A day in our life

1 Thessalonians 3:12

White Splendor

All dressed in her white splendor.
Glistening like new fallen snow . . .
Bright nervous smile, on rosy lips
she waits to hear the music flow.

The melody will take her
to a new step in her life . . .
One she feels will last forever . . .
The ever after love she blooms

Like she has never felt before . . .
He is strong and bold
Awe so gentle and loving . . .
He will be a wonderful father . . .

She will be honored to bring,
new life with her body . . .
Made from their love . . .
She will treasure their seed

She hears the music,
Takes her first step into view,
All stand as they see her . . .
Loves beauty reads on her face . . .

Making her eyes like diamonds
The light radiates with stars
all the way to the front of the church . . .
Half way it meets with one like a twin.

These lights twine as one,
Like the life together,
That is about to begin.
The rest of their lives . . .

Ecclesiastes 4:9 & 10
John 17:11

She Met Him at the Picture Show

She was such a shy young lady
Never been on a date before
She was a preacher's kid,
Her father watched like a hawk, he did

She met him at the picture show
Where her girlfriend took her in tow
He was tall lean and older
It made her become some bolder

Somehow he caught this young ladies eye
Out to meet him she would fly
They began to meet at the show quite regular
He brought along his brother for her friend

She was of the other Irish
Bold blue eyes and wavy black hair
The kind of looks that made guys stare
But she only looked at him

He wasn't sure of her heart he could win
He was just a poor building laborer
How could he ever win her favor?
But she soon told of her heart

How it was only him she wanted a part
Soon they had to tell her father
They took a while to tarry
But soon they would want to marry

Her father took it all in strife
When he asked to make her his wife
Soon after they were married
A family they would be

Two girls and boy
Three in as many years
Then ten years later, me

Jeremiah 31:3

Reason Enough to Worry

I think I must be ill

Or maybe I am Allergic

When you come into the room

My heart starts to race

The palms of my hands sweat

Then when you get closer

When I can smell your sweetness

I can't stop the showing of my teeth

The blood runs to my face

I am sure I am an idiot

I am close to foaming at the mouth

There is reason enough to worry

I've never felt this way before

It must be a heart attack

Or some other worse fate

I hope I survive this state

1 Peter 1:8

Music

I wish to hear the songs once more.
I wish the silence would end.
I would like to sing like I used to,
To hear the melody and join in

To hear the notes floating through the air,
As they dance to reach my ear.
The songs of a new love, the excitement of rock
or just a simple tune to lighten a care

But it is not to be, it doesn't work,
So I'll just write these words.
Go on as I am, all for the best,
And leave the songs to the rest . . .

But when heaven sounds
when that day comes around,
This infirmity will be set free
I'll hear then you see!

I'll hear that trumpet sound
My feet will lift
I'll leave the ground
No more on earth to hear no sound

Isaiah 29:18

True Treasures

Dreams are tomorrow's treasures

Wrapped with beautiful paper and ribbons

Waiting for you to unwrap them

But sometimes we can't move

Past the superficial beauty

Discard the outer shell

To acquire the true gift

Deuteronomy 32:34

John 4:10

Isaiah 1:23

CHAPTER 7

Come Ride in My Car

Will you come ride in my car?

We'll roll down the windows

Play like in a convertible

Let the wind whip our hair

As we get that lovers lean

Stokin' our mirror aviators

Ridin off in the sunset

With no destination in mine

Ya know everything will be fine

With you by my side, what a cool ride

When we're about to run out of gas

We'll pull under an apple tree

Just you and me, making a home

With fresh fruit of the tree

Ya, just you and me!!

Ya babe, just you and me!!

Deuteronomy 32:13

Dream Away

Who is to hear my song?

I may think deep and long

I may sing a vacant tune

Something of impending doom

Who will listen a sparrow away?

Who will give me light of day?

Will someone stop sojourn awhile

Light my face with a smile

A crowd in the room, still all alone

Mind to wonder often to roam

Travel I must to this fantasy land

Dancing footprints across the sand

Who will see that I am not here?

No one to notice I have no fear

Tiptoe the mind back now in place

No one to miss me in this rat race

Lamentations 3:28

One Hot Golden Brown French-fry

My French fries are
nice and hot
but why did they give
me this lot!

I try to save them
for later
but when I warm
they taste like leather

When I was a teen
I used to have to call
them like this
One hot golden brown

French fry, please
They called it
suggestive selling
So everyone in the store

Heard me yelling!
One hot golden brown
French fry, please
But in reality
they don't stay
that way long
cold by the end of a song!
I throw
out my fries to the birds
Here they come
in herds!

flying right over
my one hot golden brown
French fry, please.

Revelation 3:15 & 16

217

Not About Games

You dream the day your ship will come in
Some game of chance you hope to win

What kind of optimism is this fate?
While you are dreaming, it could be too late

Faith in a bottle is passed around
All drowning sorrow out on the town

She calls from the corner, How about a good time
Look around, this is what you will find

A Tear is formed from His Heavenly view
But He hasn't lost His faith in you

Will you watch for another ship?
Will you cease from the bottle to tip?

Will you let him fill your cup?
Hear the voice of Jesus look up!

The name above all names
Life is too short to play these games

Deuteronomy 30:14-16
Joshua 24:15

Boot Camp for Heaven

One Two Three Four

get yourself on bended knee

if heaven you want to see

Five Six Seven Eight

it is worth this worldly wait

to see that pearly gate

Nine Ten Eleven Twelve

the choice it is no choice at all

It is heaven or it is hell

Proverbs 6:20-23

Soothing Music

Tears fade by soothing music that caress the soul

captured by subtle illusive haunting whispers

Spell is lifted by truth raining sorrow

sunset brings a soothing reassurance

Time tells of laugher reigned by deception

printing in the dusty jewels entwined

Stress is rambling phase of life lesson

song birds bring ending to lonely

Wish draws to the core being neighborly

comments sink to the unknown mire

Smoothness satisfies the temperament naturally

I remember poems sketched in moonlight

Sunlit exchange by nightlight on the breeze

1 Samuel 16:23

Whisper

The wind blows a gentle warm breeze
The soft caw of a bird
The distant howl
The dew on the flower
A miniature image

The whisper in my heart
I love you my child
I close my eyes
Excepting the embrace
The touch brings a tear

The content welcome
Like a spring bubbling
a lost fountain in the desert
A welcome quenching
A soul so thirsty

Making for a light heart
In a torrent of earthly woe
Take me with thee I plea
I love you my Lord
I hear His whisper
"Every step I am by your side
Live your life for me."

I step to walk away
looking back not seeing him
Then I hear the wind blow
With a gentle whisper
"I'm right here . . ."

1 Kings 19:12
Hebrews 13:5

Plastic Flowers Never Die

There blooms are cast to perfect
Stems even and straight
No watering needed, No pruning
Just admire their perfect beauty

But then as time goes, and the light
Ah, the light filtering from above
It fades their plastic leaf
Taking prettiness, they have no memory
So how can they live on?

They can't be pressed in a book
Stuck in that ever erect state
Soon ownership is shifted
Then to the land fill they live
With all the other imitations

No one to preen their faded sprig
No one to cherish a cold core
No, it matters not to them
The machine will turn their grave
Dark is where they belong . . .

Ah, yet God is the creator
Even of plastic flowers
For if they never was
How would we even know?
When something was real . . .

Isaiah 28:1

Summer's Sun

I didn't expect the stars to fall
Did not hear the whispering call
I wanted to play in summer's sun
Sand beneath my feet for fun

The breath of breeze in my hair
Sauntering on without a care
I embraced the green a lass
Playing heart of youthful past

Rains of storm entered in
Caught without my canopy
Eyes a mist as monsoon pour
Unrequited heart that soar

Oh father of the whispering wind
Take my heart of aching bend
Turn it into a red rose flower
As I lean from my power

Mine is yours to keep within
Holding out this human hand
I want to play in summer's sun
Sand beneath my feet for fun

Matthew 24:29

223

Whispers of Aura

My heart beats heavy under my rib
I sense your approaching aura
A whispering wind to my soul
Dancing with the growing tide

Sunrises splashing with the waves
Reflecting like a halo above your head
Breeze ripples through dark shiny strands
Like a ghost waving in misty night

The moon mirrors in eyes so dark
Twinkling as you look my way
Balancing the moon in starlight dreams
I saunter to eye the lingering beams

I see your shadow in the mist
A delight parallel to the Heavens
My craving reels to savor your neck
As darkness kisses the sunshine

My lips reach to taste destination
Let me feel your heart to my soul
Let us then sing harmonies song
As we drift in the melody of ours . . .

Songs of Solomon 8:7

Build a Castle

I build my castle in this land
Working hard to get where I am
Oh I carry this load to build
Got to make a good yield

Wake in the morning
Tumble to bed so late
Early A.M. I have to make
But sleep don't come I am awake

I stumble to make the funds
No time to say hello, on the run
You say good bye with a sigh
But I don't hear as you go by

The bed is cold that night
I watch the window come to light
I didn't know you took flight
I didn't do anything by you right

I built this castle in the sand
The tides came in, washed away the land
Will you give me another chance?
I'll take time to dance

I'll smell the roses in your garden
Just please, I beg a pardon
I fall to my knees in agony
Dear Lord, bring my love back to me

Matthew 7:26 & 27
Ecclesiastes 1:2 & 3

Gossip

Gossip, Gossip
you don't say
who we will
pick on today!

It don't matter
if it's true
If there is something
the talk to brew!

Over coffee or tea
that's the best
conversation
you see!

It don't matter
who we hurt!
We will dig up
all the dirt!

If this is the way
you want to be seen.
If not, don't say
things mean!

Gossip, Gossip!
Everywhere!
It's harder to keep silent
than spread your fare!

So close your mouth,
don't say a word!
Keeping silent
as a bird!

Ecclesiastes 5:2

Rest Today

Rest today is what I need.

Rest today is the seed.

Rest today from all the work

Rest today from all that lurks

Rest today from my thoughts

Rest today from all the ought's

Rest today by the gentleness of God's hands

Washed away by cleansing sands . . . .

Jeremiah 6:16

Exodus 31:15

Lone Cloud

Lone cloud high in the sky

you fill my world

with shadows

as you walk by.

A bright sunshine

then changing light

you creep over the land

like a demon in the night

not lasting long

Let the Sun chase you away

because you don't belong here

on this pretty summer day!

Matthew 17:5

Hosea 6:4

I May Never Write a Sonnet

Sigh, I may never write a sonnet

But I'll keep poems in my bonnet

For a rainy, gloomy day

To chase the doom away

They'll tell of times of sunshine

Of frosted drinks of key-lime

A bobbin in the lake

Layin' in the sun to bake

Feet crossed real relaxed

Dreams drifting from a sax

Better than take me away Calgon

When everything is alright, not wrong

Proverbs 14:13

By Faith

Have we not the breath for life
Never seen but inhaled to sustain

Does not the sparrow sow, but is fed
When the wild flower blooms
Bold and beautiful

Some never seen, but there for whom?
Is it possibly all by chance

The wind blows its breath
We see it works
But never the wind

The Branches bend and break
Is it the darkness that's seen?
No it is the light that shines there

The river with fish
The air with foul
The breath we breathe
The heart to love
yes to be hurt
to feel

By chance
By Faith
By God

Hebrews 11:1

Steal My Heart

Steal My Heart,

O my soul.

Take it from my hand.

Deliver me to the

shadows of your being.

Take me to the depth

of your hearts existence.

Hide me from all that is!

Take me from this place,

to an exodus that is,

only known to us!

Ephesians 5:28

Gentle Spirit

I hear your voice saying don't fret
Our works not done just yet
I hear your voice say look up
I will fill your cup

I feel your touch gentle and warm
Letting me know you'll keep me from harm
I feel you lift this spirit so down
I just can't be sad when you are around

You come in like a gentle friend
Extending the hand you lend
Wrapping me in a spirit of love
Giving me a taste of heaven above

Filling me with your wonderful awe
Bringing me a heavenly call
To spread this feeling all around
Your heart of love to abound

Gentle spirit touch this soul
Take off this feeling of the cold
Gentle spirit, sing me a song
Making me for heaven to long . . .

Psalm 18:30-37

Gentle Sea

Looking upon the gentle sea

With dreams of you and me

Folded in your arms,

Loved by all your charms . . .

Safe from the world of harms . . .

I know this is where

I've always been meant to be . . .

Because in your arms

I am free . . .

Deuteronomy 33:27

The Visit

Pull up a chair

tell me a tale

Be it of God

with his wonderful flair

What grand adventure

do you recollect to share?

I need a parable

to ward off the care

Men blowing trumpet

a woman beautiful and fair

A tale of a lost country

of bounty, void of bare

Cleansed in a river

of mud so brown

A beautiful Garden

flowering abound

A bubbling spring

would heal to the touch

if you couldn't reach it,

it wouldn't mean much

A beautiful land

All due to inherit

Even streets that is gold

I'm told is up there

You see I am weak

I won't be here someday

I need to know

Heaven will be what they say

Colossians 1:5

By Your Side

Look into my eyes

Tell me my words are a surprise

I want to be by your side

This love I can no longer hide

When I'm around you

My heart does a flip and a flop

It's a feeling that I can't stop!

Makes me want to do 80's pop

I'm just a silly kinda boy

Acting like a windup toy

When you're around I have such joy

Please help this kinda crazy boy

Put me out of my misery

Please don't play the mystery

You know my heart is in your hands

I want to be in all your plans!

Hebrew 13:5

Whisper in My Ear

Whisper in my ear . . .
Tell me you are there.

A soft breeze blew
But you didn't hear . . .

Show me in the sky . . .
If you are way up high . . .

The lightening flashed right by
You shook your head and let out a sigh.

Show me in this life . . .
You heard a baby cry . . .

You stopped and pondered why.
Could God be just a lie?

Show me some kind of sign.
A crocus peeps through the snow.

I sent you all of this,
But you still didn't know.

1 Kings 19:11 & 12

Sometimes I Don't Understand

Sometimes I don't understand, what is in your plan.
Help me to appreciate your love,
Help me to understand,
Help me to realize,
Help me to appreciate your love.

When my life is so confused,
and the future I don't know,
Help me to appreciate your love.
Help me to understand,
Help me to realize,
Help me to appreciate your love.

When there just don't seem to be an end,
and the figures just don't work.
Help me to appreciate your love,
Help me to understand,
Help me to realize,
Help me to appreciate your love.

When my heart is growing weak,
and my health is in your hands.
Help me to appreciate your love,
Help me to understand,
Help me to realize,
Help me to appreciate your love.

Psalm 119:34

My Obnoxious Little Fur

Don't be obnoxious my little fur
Rubbing thy hair to tangle and purr
Winking those deep green eyes
Plying claws in ignoring skin

You render thy cute with aim
Oh poor victims concentration lame
Straight arrow to heart thy blow
Slithering through flesh and blood

No mind the thy injury carcass depth
Delighting for thy own attentive wealth
Feeding thy amorous intention riveting
Purring delighted happiness melodies

Looking into your wanting greens
Untamed habitual heart perceives
You too a victim to this stretch
As I pull you into hearts arm tamed

Genesis 3:1

Bird Of Prey

Lift your wings you bird of prey

No more will he see the light of day

Hid behind a woman's' breast

Till taken out by the best

Death no more by his hand

Ridden from us in this land

Oh, the tears of remembered sorrow

As of yesterday's time we borrow

Others may attack this bird of prey

But remember we're the proud USA!

Isaiah 49:24

Live With Elvis

He moves his legs to the rhythmic beat
Holding tight to the silver mic
His slicked back black bang
Falls over his swaying forehead

He pulls seductively at his scarf
Wrapped loosely around his neck
Working it in his ring clad hand
He murmurs the words love me tender

The crowd roars and pushes forward
Trying to get closer to the stage icon
Arms flail in a lariat movement
He tosses the scarf to worshiping arms

The screaming crowd now crushed to the front
He moves to a spellbinding pounding beat
Captivating every fan with
A threat to stay off his blue suede shoes

Sweat drips down his forehead to his squinted baby blues
He grinds both his guitar and the motion from his hips to toes
Ending with a low bow and
Thank you Thank you very much

The crowd roars and takes the stage
His body guards move in holding them back
He makes his exit to his waiting limo
Time for the king to retreat

Songs of Solomon 4:1

This is a Test

When the trials get heavy

And the road seems low

There are some things

I think you should know

This is a test

A school if you would

To see what our use will be

In another neighborhood

One with no bounds

No dips in the road

One where we will help

Someone else

With their load

Oh the perks

On wings we will fly

With a Sword of His Spirit

As we float on high

James 1:3 & 4

Mike's Black Angus Burger

Go to the local grocery store
Buy a pound of Black Angus or more

Look for a tomato that is the reddest
Now find the freshest lettuce

Making sure the buns are nice and soft
I know this is work, don't scoff

Onions and pickles make it best
Double Colby Cheese to finish the test

Pat them out for your dear
Have a mug of root beer

I like to use a little seasoning
Taste to see the reasoning
Onion powder, garlic too
A little Mrs. Dash will do

I like to use a little salt
To use too much is to fault
Mix the seasoning with the meat
Now to grill this special treat

Four minutes on each side
Is the time to abide?
You will joyfully lick your lips
If you follow all my tips!!

Job 6:6

Enchanted By the Muse

Enchanted by the muse you play

I can't see the light of day

You twist my thinking all around

To your thoughts though unsound

I can't see reality

I can only see what you make me be

With your darken deadly ploy

You take away all my joy

You bring me to a world fancy

Where everything is a fantasy

You give me material possession

Leading me with darken passion

I'm a puppet in your hand

I dance to your idyllic band

Save me from this human throw

The one I suffer here below

2 Corinthians 10:3-5

Going Home

Nothing feels like going home
Missed time of being away
Hugs from missed loved ones
The smile on their face
Home cannot be replaced

It's our comfort
When we've been away
A time to relax away the day
A Favorite blanket
Or color of the room

The taste of food you long for
Your favorite recipe
The familiar road turn
That lets you know
You'll be there soon

It's a little taste of heaven
Down here on earth
Sometimes it takes
Some time away
For you to know what it was worth

There's a longing in your heart
To join loved ones
On the other shore
You know as they leave you
They'll be waiting by the door

Yes there are Golden streets
And a pearly gate
The Bible tell us this
But it's the longing
for that warm embrace
The most, is what you wish

Hebrews 11:10-16

Stage Fright

Sweating, time to take the stage
applaud would erupt
Crescendo of laud sound
dimples would wrinkle
face would be brighter than
the stage light illumination

All is but a thought
I cower on the chair
Words held tight
Lest I forget
Ink running together
From the sweated hands

My name is called
I trip, grabbing the stand
looking out to bulging eyes
Oh that familiar lump
Coming to my throat
Maybe I will choke to death
Before the croak proceeds

Words flow in sound
I keep going though
don't know what I am saying
I finish, silence echoes
filling the room
with melancholy

Psalm 27:1

CHAPTER 8

I'll Meditate

Flowers adorn on the table with flair

But those who set them aren't there

Where do they prefer to set?

In front of the shiny screen that's lit

No time to talk about their day

They know what their majesty says

No time to look at the sky so fair

Nor can they listen to weather there

No time for the bird at the window seat

They'd miss the sports defeat

The laughter heard from the other room

Where shows some silly sponge cartoons

I'll set here at the table to meditate

For God's voice I'll humbly wait

Psalm 25:5

Morning Games

The sun is in a game of tag

With a heavy cloud

It tries to out run the mirth

Gets tackled in the bout

A glimmer of a hand stretched

Pushes at gray clout

A shimmer of a ray is shown

In the round about

Matthew 17:5

Beyond Life's Path

Oceans play through my fingers

As I dream of last night's kiss

My eyes stare at blue skies

I hear the lore of a distant song

The whisper of blossoms in the wind

May rains fall to sear the burning fire?

The dew glistens from the rays of sun

Solitude dreams her lovely song

Darkness is lifted in this forest

Warmth floods me with dreams

The green grass is as eternal I feel

Love lightens path with faith and trust

Who knew a rainbow would wait

At the end of this lighted path

I breathe in the welcome of love

I rejoice in the dawn a new day

2 Timothy 4:7-8

Reflection of a Morning

I set alone
Me and my thoughts
The dreams of this moment
Over shadow the ought

The sand at my feet is warm
between my toes
Where this dream
will take me only God knows

A glimpse of the Sunrise
Reflects on the ocean
The water splashing
Is the only motion

A Seagull sweeps by
In search of a fish
Life always this peaceful
Is only a wish.

Soon all will be awake
Ready for their day
I'll reflect on this moment
Throughout my long day

Isaiah 58:8

The Church in the Cornfield

The Church in the Cornfield

A gentle breeze flows through the cornfield,

The soft gray breaks the golden amber

It peeks whispering through with beams

An attempt to touch the very God that gives

Most days it stands like an ordinary structure

Sunday, voices spring from its doors and windows

Angelic breath flowing with the breeze

People come from near and far to worship

A desire to touch their creator

Their desire, to touch His hemmed garment

His word is spoken in the pulpit

The message inspired,

Will it reach the hearts?

That comes to this building

The messenger can only do what's asked

Leave the rest to God . . .

Ephesians 5:27

Somewhere Over the Rainbow

Somewhere over the Rainbow
Only where angels dare to go

A dream of no more sorrow
Of a perfect place to lie low . . .

The snow won't freeze,
my brittle fingers . . .

I won't look for food
in a dumpster . . .

Won't be a folded box
to pillow my head . . .
I wonder,
how I got here.

But it was just,
a few mistakes or so . . .
Somewhere over the rainbow
only where angels dare to go

Is just around the corner . . .
I hear them sing my song . . .
Somewhere over the rainbow
Just a few mistakes or so . . .

Romans 5:5-8

Path

The broken rhinestone sets on the counter
A reminder of dreams left unfilled
I beautiful gem left with scars
Beautiful yet with its uneven parts

The heart is an amazing thing
It can reroute its vital life giving blood
Given you more time on earth
Opening new passages

Still parts would be dead
Is it not what was intended?
That we have a choice
Like a monopoly being played out?

Watch and protect
Pray and choose wise
For you can't detect
What in your life lies?

Ask the Lord
To give you a hand
Do what's accord
For him to stand

Proverbs 3:1-35

Morning

I lay my head to slumber

I think of friends

On the other side

In a place where the sun

Lights morning

To my night

I dream for them

A wonderful day

Touched

With

Love

Laughter

Peace

Revelation 21:3 & 4

The View

Sunbeam light reflects smiling color

Glistening in white capped ocean waves

Peeking clouds that try hard unsuccessfully

To block sun in its grace only being glorified

The white caps splash with tiny prisms

Throwing about angels dancing with rainbows

Mist meandering back to the heavens throne

With each roar from a wild tune playing tide

The gold kisses the ocean with a color

One that was mixed with feather tip wings

The photographer a mere inspired mortal

Gifted with an eye touched from heaven

Psalm 27:4

Psalm 90:17

Revelation 15:2

Folded Memory

Sun streams into the room

Coffee perking aromas delight

A sigh escapes from dry lips

Night is folded in memories

The soft touching

The love felt

No spoken words needed

An endless kiss

Love long waited for

Entwined bodies nestled

Together as God intended

Cleaving as one . . .

Genesis 2:24

Tommy Cat

He goes through the fields

proud of himself.

He has a confidence that

belittles his size.

He blends very well,

with the gold in the fields.

In prey of a victim.

That is not as wise.

His moves are so settle.

Not a thing can hear.

As he swiftly creeps,

their caught, by surprise!

Psalm 124:6 & 7

God

I feel His presence,

I feel ashamed,

I feel humbled,

I feel accepted,

I feel peace,

I feel grace,

I feel yearning,

I feel passionate,

I feel alive,

I feel intense,

I feel immortal,

I feel elevation,

I feel, GOD.

1 Corinthians 12:6 & 15:28

Ephesians 1:23

Trippin' On the Train

I had a tooth ache the other day

I didn't feel like driven

On to the train I sway!

The Doctor said "it is an abscess tooth

This won't take long, it's already loose!"

Let's get you a little laughing gas!

Well he lowered the gas, it wasn't a laugh

All the dreams came up from my past!

It was all over, for soon did I leave

I got to the port, not quite sure how

Because everything was pretty WOW!

The image out the window whizzed on by

In dancing psychedelics and apple pie

I wish I remembered the entire ride,

Cause the first step was a tumbler!

Psalm 2:4

Psalm 126:2

The Date

Do you have time for a cup of tea?
Time to set to share with me?
I lifted from the velvet set up
She lifted a delicate floral cup

I set back with a sigh
Watching hands on the clock go by
She filled the delicate vessel
As time in my mind I wrestled

I had so much on my plate
Couldn't we make it another date?
Something in her eyes made me set
Maybe I'd visit just a little bit

She brought in her china platter
Filled to the brim with matter
Bite sizes of this and that
I stopped and removed my hat

A smiled moved across her wrinkled face
I pushed away the Urge to pace
She looked at me all stressed
Smoothed her clothes so overdressed

She opened her mouth and began a tale
My face I knew grew very pale
But as I listened, my heart begin to bloom
Her Story of love, adventure filled the room

I was mesmerized by her soft voice
In her adventure I rejoiced
As she ended her story of wit
Of my cup I drained the last sip

I told her we'd do this again soon
I got up to leave the room
She ask, "How about same time next week?"
I said, "That is a date I'll keep!"

Proverbs 19:23

262

Lost Song

I sing a song of morning damp

Face shining with a tear

I miss my summer days

The ones my heart holds near

The fun of youthful runs

In a nearby field

The kind of all-day fun

Youthful spirits yield

I tumble, and then I laugh

At their antic game

A swan dives for a bath

I wonder at the fame

Oh, wasted year

Come back to this lost soul

I feel it is random fear

Father time does take his toil.

Ecclesiastes 12:1

Crossing

Stepping on the stones of life

Crossing through the river

Sometimes we fall right in

When flood reaches the sky

Covering the stony path

The jump at times too long

The stones so far away

Will I ever get to the land of dry?

Psalm 66:12

In the Shadow of Sunflowers

I paint here in the shadow

The great Sistine Chapel

Lumen before my muse

Oh my muse sets here

Oh Van Gogh

Painting sunflowers,

Sunflowers of all things!

Flowers grown

For the seeds to be eaten

My muse

Where does it grow?

In the night my dreaming

It whispers, write it down.

I am here again . . .

In great shadows

painting my sunflowers . . .

Psalm 102:11

John 14:18

Dreams of Tomorrow

The grass tickles my feet
barefoot we walk
We spread a blanket
To set and talk

I'll lay my head on your shoulder
we dream of the life
We'll soon have together
When I become your wife

We'll have a little cottage up on the hill
Making love whenever we will
We won't wait long, children to bear
Your blue eyes, my blond hair and fair

I'll tend to my rose garden
While you work through the day
When you're home in the evening
We'll take time to play

You'll leave in the morning
we'll hate to part
But while you're away,
you'll be in my heart

1 Corinthians 7:32-34

Be Encouraged

When life sends an uphill lane

Filled with shadows and endless pain

Look up to an infinite showering

From an Omnipotent Shining love

Raise your head up high

Listen to the birds, they tweet

He's taking care of them

See the dew He sent the flower

For you he gave His own breath

His mouth touched your lips

Would He not do yet for you?

The one held close to His heart

Matthew 6:28

The Nightmare

I listen to the still night

Glissade slow around

Light glistens through the window

No noise to be found

I close my eyes to see the morn

as my mind wonders to ought

Scared I jump in terror

for all the pain I've got

I hide it in the day light

it's not easily seen

but in the night it comes about

when sleep is in between

If only I could jet this nightmare

Send it back to where it came

the hell it's opened to me

I'll never be the same

Job 7:4

Storm of the Heart

Whispering rain falling on my face

Hide away the tears without a trace

Lightning flashing long across the sky

Making me remember the night you said goodbye

Wind rushes in blowing away my mind

Leaving lost memories behind

Clouds forming high in the sky above

Makes me yearn for times we had love

Stormy nights of passion spent in your arms

Wrapped in your loving embrace and enchanted charms

But forces beyond our love worked to keep us apart

When you packed your bag to go, you took along my heart

Luke 4:18

Jeremiah 17:14

Where Angels Are Birthed

Her elegant dress of white morning cloud

Her head illuminating held high and proud

Her voice strong soft voice call you there

She comes to take you to a land of fair

I grasp her hand and away we both flew

Over rivers and mountains tall and blue

To a land on the other side of the earth

To a land where angels are birthed

Speaking of other worlds faraway

Places she said I would visit someday

Dream the living I never thought to meet

All this to grasp was quite a feat

But somehow I knew it was all for me

This new land and life to someday see

She took me back to my home below

The smile on her face all I needed to know

Psalm 103:20

Matthew 4:11

Listen To His Voice

Trying our faith makes us stronger
Praying through takes longer
He always gives us choice
If we will listen to his voice

Seek me who are down hearted
I was not the one who parted
You stood up and walked away
When I wanted you to stay

I wanted to hear from your heart
I not wanting to tear you apart
I hoped you'd bring it to me
I will be here to listen to your plea

I've always been very close
Treasured you more than those
I'll be here at your will
When you have time, be still

Like A soft and gentle spirit
You must take time to hear it
Don't rush through the day
Without listening to the words I say . . .

Psalm 24:6-10
Psalm 17:3
1 Peter 1:7

271

Car Rider

She was driving to work one night
The sun setting in her rear mirror
When a visitor in her car should appear
What next took hold of her was pure fear!

Out of fear she pushed hard on the accelerator
Saw there flashing lights of the exterminator
Her visitor ran and hid out of sight
As she told the officer of her plight!

Would he feel horror and compassion!
He rolled over, laughed without ration!
He opened car door, found the hiding predator
Hiding in a crack, legs showing on her car floor

Eight legs and a fuzzy body lay in the gravel
To no more interrupt her travel
Smilingly the officer advised no more flight!
Slow down and have a good night!

The officer now was her best hero
She'd watch how she drove to and fro
For her knight in shining armor
Dragon and spider killer to honor

Psalm 91:13

Reflecting Our Love

The breeze softly wrestles the window curtain

I feel your sleeping breath kiss my cheek

I reflect the love your heart brings

Cherishing our shared love

Wrapping arm tight around bringing you closer

You stir a bit snuggling in loves embrace

Right here is where I want to be

For the rest of my life

Watching the breeze run through the curtain

With your breaths kiss on my cheek

I snuggling in your arms

Reflecting my love . . .

1 John 4:16-21

My Love

I look all around me,

All the hurt that I see

Broken dreams and heart aches

I feel blessed it's not me.

You are hidden deep in my heart.

My lover, my companion, my friend . . .

Just like the vows we took.

I know we will be together

Until the very end!

Matthew 28:19 & 20

I Lift My Hands to You

I lift my hands to you Oh Lord

You are the one to be adored

You take my trembling hands in yours

I know it's me that's adored

Why is it you love me

Like you do

You say, I'm your child

But I am so wild

I need your warm embrace

It slows my worldly pace

I get lost in you

For you are so true

I dance to your love song

It is with you I belong

So take me away I pray

To another time and day

Psalm 50:23

Flying High

She is flying high today

Fluttering about

Dancing with the clouds

Twirling around the hill tops

Skating with the wind

Smiling at the sunrise

Laughing at the baby birds

As they try their wings

Loving them with encouragement

Listening to the wind whistle

It plays a tune through the tree

Swaying with the meadow

Can you see her dancing?

Can you hear the music play

Can you smell the flowers?

See the smile on her face

Feel the enchantment

In your gift of the day

Psalm 103:5

Sailing Through

Won't you touch me Lord?

I need to feel you close.

Won't you take my hand?

Help me through this land.

This is not my home.

I know I don't belong.

Just like the song.

My ship is sailing through!

The Journey on these waters

sure can be tough.

Help this weakened soul

To make it when it's rough . . .

Psalm 46:1

Sleepless

I wander in the room of lonely

Twinkling light glisten the window

My tired eyes roam the ceiling

Nothing but white wash to grasp

Car lights dance the room like imps

Walking the rooms evasive perimeter

I wish to sleep in dreams of dreams

Mind wondering to the ills of ifs

Oh tiredness, take me to that land

The one I want to meander to walk

Eyes rubbed red numb heart drifts

The only response to my plea

There it is bounding about

Another light at my window

Daniel 6:18

Summer Love

You flew in on a wisp in June

Lighting my path on a summers moon

My heart fluttered when you came that day

Chasing my dark cloud's away

Spent our summer playing in the sand

Jeweled seashells spread out on the land

Sparkled like diamonds in the August day

Summers reminder when you'd fly away

The hedge lay unspoken as summer passed

A summer romance that could not last

The picture perfect, love it seems

Only a tale, ending with summer dreams

Matthew 24:32

CHAPTER 9

Sent From Above

Were you just an angel?

Sent from above?

With words of mercy,

Showing us His love?

Did he send you down here?

To show us the way,

To make heaven our home,

Some coming glorious day!

Was this your assignment?

To love us down here,

Help us along with,

A heart full of care

He knows what we go through,

Each and every day

He knows we needed a friend

To help along the way!

Hebrews 13:1

Endless Heaven

If time could be compared

An inch here on earth

Compared to endless miles in Heaven

Our earthly time is oh so short

We must be busy doing God's work

Each storm we must travel

Has its purpose, though we may not see

Preparing us for what heavens life to be

When you think it's really tough

When the oceans waves are rough

Look up to ask for His hand

It's stronger than any earthly man . . .

Psalm 84:10

Conflicting Thoughts

Not knowing what words to use
Where did I lay my muse?
Maybe I don't know how to feel
I need to make my life real

Conflicting thoughts scramble my brain
All of this can really drain
I hate the lunacy of society
It is such a malediction to propriety

Why must we follow a system?
That sometime lacks for wisdom
Ha, social acceptable behavior
Why can't we do whatever we favor?

I want to be a kid again run and swing
pretend to have wings
I want to be bold
Not just do what I'm told

I don't think I am understood
Maybe it's my second childhood
I don't want to go to jail
Ha! No one would post my bail!

Psalm 71:1-5

Another Day

Teapot whistles bout dry again
The burner top so hot
Cracking my egg,
The pan sizzles turned off,
It cooks to perfection

I pour the half cup water left
To drink a bit a tea
Going through the pain
To stave off the growl

That there game nags me
I can hear it call
Even with deaf ears
Forget and make a life

The smile curves at the irony
The little puppet
Roams around the virtual
Simply happy for someone
To play at the controls

I go through motions
Trying not to think
But my mind wanders
Where did that dream go . . . ?

Ecclesiastes 7:10

The Keeper of the Keys

Humans housed like animals, for crimes of life

For choices made they now live in strife

They all have a story, some sadly true

They are much the same as me and you

The keeper of the keys I am

But in another time I was like them somehow

It is choices in life we make

Choice that will tell our very fate

The keeper of the keys I am

But only by grace

For at another time

For me it was a different pace

I choose to leave

That life behind

Before it became a crime

Oh, the keeper of the keys I am

But only by God's grace

Galatians 5:1

Poetry! Poetry!

Poetry, Poetry Everywhere

Poetry, poetry everywhere!

Poetry, poetry in my hair!

There is poetry under my seat!

There poetry at my feet!

Did you see it floating there?

Why it was raining from the air

It was jumping on my melon

Did you see it stand a yellin!

Oh, the words they make me beat!

They use to be a pleasant treat

So much poetry in my head!

I can't even get to bed!

Psalm 119:49-50

Pizza for Breakfast

Breakfast Medleys
from the night before
Rolling the dough kneading it firm
Working with the hands
Using finger tips press in the pan
Red and plump tomatoes
Diced with a knife to tidbit pieces
Delight the taste bud quit nice
Shedding the mozzarella
Working back and forth
Drying the oregano
to flutter on the top
An artist of succulence
That lay on the counter
Hot vapors release
When the oven door opens
Mouth-watering aroma
Escaping from the seams
The mixture of pleasure
Waters the tongue
The tastes they explode
Trapping the senses
Moans from the mouth
Driving hunger senseless

Psalm 136:25

A Troll

There once was a beautiful land
Where every written word could stand
But around came a troll called Mr. Petty
He chased away every Tom, Dick and Betty!

When he seen what a nuisance he could be
He hid behind every flowering tree
Soon there wasn't anyone left in the land
Without the care it turned to sand

Watch don't let trolls take your muse
They will saunter in with saddest blues
They always love to bring on drama
What they leave behind smells like llama

Genesis 18:20-21

The Call

I request you to go to a land far away.

Will you heed this call, go where I say.

Will you stay where you are?

chose not to go far?

Will you go where hardships aren't easy?

I watch you struggle

with all that you have . . .

You set in your house

With your fatted calf . . .

I request you to do,

the work that needs done.

Will you ignore the call?

and go on the run?

My head is bowed low.

As I see it is hard . . .

You look out the window

the window is barred

Matthew 20:16

Romans 11:29

1 Corinthians 1:26-27

Hannah's Muse

The diamond enchantment in her hand

It held the truths to no man's land

Where dreams and hopes were locked away,

Where they are collected to stay

Until a dreamer comes with the key

Then a story they would be

Rising up in verses of muse

In the light of writes and views . . .

Isaiah 22:22

Matthew 16:19

Where Have All the Children Gone

Where have all the children gone
The play grounds never used

The running, the hide and seek
Counting and laughing in two's!

In its place a lighted screen
Friends of cyborg space

No more little tree house
No more clubs or meeting place

The basket balls bounce in the wind
The swings flow with the breeze

No more rolling in the grass
down the hill, with grass stain knees

Rover looking hopeful, at the door
While they feed a virtual pet

No need for an umbrella
They never go outside to get wet

But in front of the PC tube
Is where they will stay

Hypnotized by this silver screen
Is where they want to play?

Matthew 19:14
Ecclesiastes 7:10

Missing You Poet

Were you just an angel?
Sent from above,
With words of wonder,
Shown us with love

Did God send you down here?
To show us the way?
How to get our rhyme on,
In a flowing way!

Was this your assignment?
With your heart felt charm?
To express what we're feeling,
With pencil not harm!

You opened our minds
With all that you wrote.
Like a song of a song bird,
Singing from above.

You helped the words call us,
You did it with love.
Psalm 119:103
John 14:26

Telephone Love

Ring, Ring telephone ring

Sing, Sing

The song I set for the tone

I know it's you on my phone

Watch to see if it might be

The picture I want to see

The one that says

You're calling me

I hope, I pray,

That you will call today

I just want to hear

Whatever you say

I don't care what others might say

I just want to be with you today!

Acts 2:39

Truest Friend

What would I do without your love?

What would there be without above

Just a cold and lonely world

Where would I be without the hope?

Where would I go without our talks?

Just a cold and lonely girl

I'm so glad that I have you

I'm so glad you love me too!

Jesus you're the truest friend

That God could ever send . . .

Ephesians 2:4-6

Memories

Memory takes me back
Oh if time be what to lack
All smiles while holding hands
Listening to 45's of rock bands

My head rest beneath your chin
I always thought we would win
But time was not on our side
The young love took a dive

Dreams of a cottage with tiny feet
A war that called for you to defeat
You wanted us to follow the band
Then the call came from Uncle Sam

The life it took you far away
Until from me you went astray
We both too young to endure
We didn't keep our love pure

Born of cheating came the wrath
Sending you down another path
What would we have been today?
If from the heart we didn't stray

Proverbs 25:19

Lonely and Blue

The distant chime of the tower clock

Setting here alone on the dock

Feeling like there is no one in the world but you

Wondering why you are so blue

Is there no one a word to share

Feeling all alone and bare

Thinking my friends have all parted and gone

Is there something I did that's wrong??

Isaiah 51:2

Psalms 9:10

Psalms 42:9

Peach Preserves

I walk this path opal pale
How did I set foot on this assail
Clothed in grandeur I nor' seen
Never before my eyes beheld

Whispering hues by starlight night
Sparkling waves cast crystal light
Ocean surge lapping my feet
Trilling galls call in their flight

Open my bag from the scrap café
Set on a rock to put on display
What is inside yet to bestow
Oh, the jewels for queen devour

Grand artist has pulled out His spread
The movie plays over my head
I touch my lips with day old bread
Spread with some left peach preserves

Complain I not, for my soul is full
His gift in colossal heavenly pull
I raise my hands in blissful merit
Thanking God for all I have inherit

Psalm 95:2

The Love of a Book

Awe, the happiness
the wonderment,
A finished tale
one that has weaved

Its words through the soul
Oh, the fancies that has
run through the mind
at the author's pen!

The play of drama
unwinding its plot
with a touch of humor
a note of sadness
all is part of the dance.

They prance about
in a tale of wits.
The banter of
the relationship is laid out

The excitement was built
to a conclusion of
two souls being entwined.
Dreaming together in a path
of unmistakable love . . .

Isaiah 34:16

Rambling Thoughts

I do not like my thoughts
Ramblings of ought
Full of thoughts
Different directions

Rivers of clouds
Rippling in sunsets
Lost with a GPS
With an unobtainable address

Turn right
Turn left
Recalculating
Approaching destination

Turn around, missed turn
But I don't have reverse
Around and around I go
On a one way street

The wrong way
Red and blue lights flash
But it doesn't matter
In this Alice's land

The rabbit has the time
The man in the box
Can tell me where to go
I can tell the officer

My GPS told me to turn
down this road
Recalculating . . . recalculating . . .

Proverbs 8:35
Matthew 7:8

God's Essence

I stand here watching the sea
in and out the waves flow with my breath.

Like it has a life of its own
I hear her voice, old as time.

I listen to the calling gulls
Hoping for a peeping fish

The tide rolls out,
Splashing across rocks and leaving shells

Tiny shells glisten at the sun's touch
like a treasure of diamonds touching the eye.

The clouds in the distance meet the water
like there is no start or beginning.

The waves wash in and out over my feet.
As I press a path in the sand

A breeze prisms the water
a salty mist touching my lips

The sea sings like a soft lullaby
I close my eyes savoring the symphony

I open my eyes to a glimpse of orange
as the sun starts it's descend

Kissing the water with jewels
Fit for a queen gift

I cherish the magical essence
Given to me by my God

Mark 11:22-26

Birthing a Loving Cocoon

One day we hope to see you soon

But now you're wrapped in a loving cocoon

Where you can be nurtured and grow

Waiting for a personality God to bestow

Little fingers an artist touch

Lips to sing a song

A mind to imagine all possibilities

Feet and toes to tag along . . .

But most important in all your growth

A heart that brings forth love

John 3:5-8

Faded Glory

She bloomed her grander

Swinging her fancy gown

When all the others

Wear their faces down

Struck down by Mr. Frost

Cutting with a swaying sword

She held on to the last

Fancying his lacy linen

For all a soul to view

Displaying red velvet coat

Infrequent by very few

Amid the fade leaf

Hung tight to browning bush

Dream yesterday's enchantment

For it is nonetheless a wish

Songs of Solomon 2:1

Isaiah 35:1-2

Matthew 6:29

My Heart Misses

It is hard to let go
It may be a habit
It may be from the heart
It is always hard
When two people part

The kinship they shared
Doesn't just end
They shared much
From start to end
Two hearts that blend

But it always ends
Expectations not met
I haven't seen any
That has lasted yet
Don't linger a bet

The silence turns on
Or maybe turns off
Understandings lost
Lofty promises fade
Shiny stars fail to parade

It doesn't change the void
Leaving has left
It all is said
Under the breath
My heart misses you

Jeremiah 31:13

Blink

Blink, blink

Why is the water insistent?

Blink, blink

I try to pull it back

Blink, blink

Strangely it has its own mind

Streaming down my face

Dripping from my chin

Drip, drip

Job 16:20

A Fishy Tale

Poor Ole Jonah, swallowed by a whale
this is quite the fishy tale.

God's love for His people is still the same.
Even when we stand in stain

Whatever it takes to see you through
That is what He'll inevitably do!

He called Jonah to the task,
but Jonah chose to run very fast

God knew Jonah was the one,
But Jonah thought it not in fun

Jonah took a ship to flee!
But God is God, even over the sea!

The captain told Jonah to rise and pray
That they might live another day

It is him that we will cherish
Please tell your God don't let us perish

Jonah prayed, but continued as he pleased.

So they threw him in the seas!

The Lord prepared for him a fish.

But this was not for tasty dish!

He put Jonah in the fish's belly

told him to quit the dally!

God spoke to Jonah in that fish

To tell him of his loving wish . . .

That all his people needed to know.

Just how much He loves them so . . .

Even though at first he grumbled

In that fish he became humbled . . .

God had the fish spit him out!

That he would put away the doubt

Through the love that God spoke

With Jonah's help the people awoke

Jonah 1-4

Touching Gift

Touch for touch the feel of love

Ascending from heaven above

Reaching for a hand raised high

Spirit fire don't pass me by

I need you for this soul of blue

Your touch of love is very true

Filling me with your might

Making my world feel alright

I need to know there's more than here

This I'll feel when you draw near

Touch for touch I feel your love

Holy Spirit gift from above

Psalm 51:10-12

Time

Wading through the memories

all just a bit of time . . .

It seems like yesterday.

But now it's all behind

Yesterday it seemed like

tomorrow wouldn't come.

But now I wish for

yesterday to rerun.

Don't waste your life

on yesterday.

And what it should have been.

To use tomorrow's,

time on yesterday,

would be a sin . . .

Deuteronomy 32:7

Ecclesiastes 12:1

A Cinderella Dream

Oh to be a fledgling again
To walk hand in hand
While sharing cotton candy
Listening to carousel music
Riding on a great white stallion

Dreaming of my prince charming
Oh there's a beautiful garden
Watching your smiling face
While you tackle the rose bush
To fetch for me a flower

It's called the Cinderella Syndrome
I've had it for years
Time slips away
We all must grow up
But the dreams they don't

I still dream, dancing in the moon light
My ball gown sweeps across the room
I dream, happy days filled with laughter
A loves night filled with enchantment
How can you miss a dream . . . ?

Proverbs 13:12

Whistling Blue

Tears fall for what you must go through

But God grant He'll see you through

A healing prayer is sent your way

Morning love through end of day

Feel his mighty helping hand

In the spirit to endless sand

Bringing you to healthy days

Wondering along in His loving ways

Encouraging you with each new step

Lighting the path to dreams not yet

Bringing love beyond what's you

Flying beyond the whistling blue

Malachi 4:2

Candy Man

You ask me if I wanted to play

I didn't know I'd grow up that day

In your pocket was chocolate candy

I know now why you had it handy

Then when you came to my room

I'd be asleep but I'd wake up soon

You so gently handled me

But when you left I felt empty

I thought it was what everyone did

So my tears in the pillow I hid . . .

Job 30:8

Psalms 127:3

Psalms 27:10

CHAPTER 10

Glimpse of Heaven

Glorious beams shine through the clouds

With sun beams descending from Heaven

Like bright angel wings touching earth

Lighting the dark path with their halos

A holy celestial feeling radiates within

Like heaven kissing the mere earth

With a touching glow from her presence

Listen close lest you hear Heavenly choirs

Dimensions are beyond what can be counted

Like rain drops from the sun caressing earth

My mind wonders is it time for heavens descend

I watch to see if heaven's door will open its gate

But as I meander on I realize it is not to be yet

We must continue to carry on a while longer

I know what a glorious gift of glimpse I was given

One I will have painted in my heart and mind forever

Psalm 14:2

John 1:51

Is There Any More

I'm in love with the word romance
Where men slew dragons
And massaged your back
Vases are full colorful

Not with the nose dive dishes
And the listening ear
Oh how did work go dear?
life as a domestic engineer

The smell of fried chicken
As he hits the door
This is good meatloaf
Is there any more

Is this all I signed up for
Open a book
I grand adventure awaits
I crawl in the fantasy

The door now is open
To all that is there
I am the star
Of this, adventurous tale!

Luke 12:15

The Forbidden Fruit

She longed to touch it

That which was forbidden

Why was it the most beautiful fruit in the garden?

It was like it called her name, "Eve"

Like the branches reached out to her

Reaching to embrace her

She could almost taste of the juicy fruit

Cool to her lip

Lips that now felt parched

No one was here

No one was watching her

No one would know

She faced that which beckoned

Did it just turn her way?

Was it possible?

Did this tree have life?

She took a step its way

The limb's waved to her

Like the arms of her Adam

Calling her to embrace

The fruit swayed

a hypnotic motion

Red plump looking like a smiling face

She reached out to touched it

It was perfect, round, red shiny skin

Cool refreshing to the touch

Before she knew what she'd done

She plucked it away from the branch

She brought it to her face

Just to smell

The breeze rustled with discouragement

It smelled sweet

Slowly she opened her mouth

Savoring the first bite

Sweet juice filled her mouth

Dripping the juices from her lips

But as they entered turning to bitter

She threw away the offender

The wind blew with a howling force

As laughing at her folly

Lightening flash over head

The cloud sighed

tears ran wild from their faces

She ran for cover

the first storm

Slashed the earth

with the force of her iniquity.

Genesis 3:1-24

The New Fall Season

I hear gentle wind whisper

I know there's more to come

The days are getting shorter

We spend less time with the sun

The trees will all lose their leaves

Colorful and bright

The sun of the day will turn

Chilly cool at night

Inside the fires burn

Take off the night chill

Soup is on the stove

We covered up the grill

The harvest of the apples

Wait to be peeled

All the summer flowers

By frost have been killed

It's the changing season

say good bye to summer fun

Fall has its own excitement

The list just goes on and on

Apple cider, pumpkins

Playing in the leaves

A pretty new sweater

Hair blown by the breeze

Enjoy this new fall season

For its short to stay

Blink before you know

Twill all blow away

Genesis 1:14

Isaiah 43:19

Not a Puppet

I'm not a puppet
There's no string
He lets me do my own thing
He doesn't have me by a hook

He lets me know His life it took
I read and learn from His book
He's my a gentle friend
Taking me by the hand

Helping me to make my stand
You see it is hard to be tall
Hard sometimes to heed His call
I try my best to give him my all

He picks me up as I fall down
Oh, I want him always around
If I look, He can be found

Galatians 5:1

Deaths by Frost

Deaths dark touching bond

Seeps through this night

Brushing life at his delight

Rending a beauty he's fond

Like an icing on a cake

But death is in his wake

All under his glaze he takes

Sneaking in behind the dew

A morning mist to frighten you

Touching deep his misty blue

There's no way to stop his sin

With Jack Frost you cannot win

Isaiah 38:18

Romans 7:5-9

I Lift My Hands to You

I lift up my hands to you
I feel your heart so true
Wrap me in your loving arms
Keeping me from earthly harms

I feel I am at heaven's gate
But I have a time to wait
You have a work for me to do
I'll do what you want me to

I'll sing your praise
Through life's worrisome haze
All the night through
If it is your wish for me to

I'll climb life's mountain
While I drink from your fountain
Every step I take talking to you
For all of your words run so true

I'll bring with me some
If they will listen and come
The journey is a curved road
While I carry a load

I lift up my hands to you
I feel your heart so true
Wrap me in your loving arms
Keeping me from earthly harms

Matthew 8:19

Waiting For You to Ask

I wait to see if you will ask

The time I spend is such a task

I comb my hair until it shines

I think about a hundred times

I pinch my cheek

In hope that you will notice

To give red color

Makeup is such a bother

I press my dress

I shined my shoes

What other tactics

Can I use

Awe a dab

Of that new flower water

With label of Au'De Bela

Hope the scent

will bring me a fella

Psalm 2:8

Iridescent Feather

Iridescent feather floating through my space
Whispering on the breeze a romantic breath

Tell me where you came, of your story flight
On my pillow dreams, as I lay tonight

I'll listen contently at your stories told
How you came to be, so beautiful and bold

Are you a relic from another earthly realm?
Of an endless fight where I nor' to see

Oh iridescent feather floating through my space
Where did you come from without trail to trace?

I watched you fall from heavens cloudless sky
Caught you in my fingertips when you floated by

I held you in my hand, straight from heaven's door
Now time to let you go, I can't hold you anymore

With my breath, I send you once again in flight
Hoping for you all the best, in everywhere you light

Psalm 68:13

327

My Shadow

I miss my shadow wasn't he just there

Half under my feet, where ever I went

If I took a walk there by my side

He saunter to walk, I couldn't hide

Bright orange his coat,

A tailor couldn't make better

Furry and soft, lovely to trace

Could touch for hours, none a waste

My walks now are few

As the cold rain falls

My last vision still haunts of your pain

Without your purrs it's not the same

Psalm 102:11

The Novel

The novel, kept reader content
Page after page turned
The story played out
Unfolding the tale

Crying together in death
Hugging through sorrow
Sharing joy in accomplishments
Holding hands in darkness

Making love in a favorite place
Being lost in storms for days
Laughing with giddiness
Even a little gossip

Most books have ending
Some end happily ever after
This ending was to be written
By the midnight dream

A candle burns bright in window
The last page was ending
Ink hovered above the page
Winds came gusting

Lights flicker casting deep shadows
Covering the moonlight
Candle smoke swirls around
Dancing forming a cloud

In the deep of the night
Distance howling lonely wolf
Cries in night like a babe
Path is lost in darkness

The page slowly turns
For the last paragraph
Last words ring in the mind
Violins play melancholy

Sky burst with thunder
A rain clap breaks the silence
Rains open tapping
Heavy on tin roof

Light flashes at the window
In the path a drowned figure
Soon to be washed away
One last time from shore

In the sunny morning
Mist will spray
the face once full happy
to read last two words

The End
Jeremiah 30:2

Rose on My Pillow

A rose on my pillow . . .
I awaken to its scent,
Just a soft reminder
Of the night we spent.

Passion of our love,
On the rumpled sheet
A sweet musical melody
Honey memories to keep.

You held me oh so tight,
For our loves sake
With such loving passion,
My skin began to bake.

I look into your eyes,
That is all it takes.
It's no wonder why,
To heart I say goodbye,

The night it plays,
Over in my mind
Like a melody sways on
From an antique music box

I dream away my day
Until your steps I hear
The rose scent whispers
Telling me you are near

Songs of Solomon 2:8

Empty Nest

When you're gone

It's a lonely song

I hear the clock

My mind goes in a shock

The house is empty

I hear no laughter

Through the halls

I set and stare at the walls

My life is oh so incomplete

Without you under feet

I look for things to do

To keep me from feeling blue

I know I must keep the pace

Until it's time to see your face

Isaiah 34:11

John 8:29

Mustard Seed Faith

Transform me that I believe
You'll take care of every need

If I just have the faith
The size of a mustard seed

After all you are the one
Who on water walked?

You're the only one
That could make a donkey talk

You opened eyes with mud
For someone that was blind

For a man that was mad
You sent the madness into swine

Why surely I can believe
You'll take care of every need

Help me have the faith
In your loving plan

Even though sometimes it's hard
For this mere moral to understand

Matthew 17:20

The Pumpkin

The Pumpkin said to the vine
You are holding my lifeline

The vine said to the dirt
You are my best perk

The root said to the rain
I am so glad you came

The sun said to the plant
You were once a little scant

Now it is time to let go
Your time has ended to grow

Cut a smile in that face

Put those seeds in a safe place
Light the path on this hallowed night

To keep the children from darken fright
You have won this plight of fame

Now Jack-o-lantern is your name

2 Peter 3:18
Isaiah 53:2

Yonder the Wheat Winds Blow

Yonder where the wheat winds blow

A break in the meadow where flowers grow

There is a clearing all our own

Where our kisses have been sown

Take my hand, lead the way

Until the braking of the day

Hold me in your ribbed embrace

Until my heart your love encase

I need the enclosure of your arms

Shielding me from earthly harms

I'll close my eyes and dream to go

Yonder where the wheat winds blow

Deuteronomy 33:27

Psalms 147:12-18

Psalms 81:16

Be a Battleship

Be a battleship at the gates of Hell

Be a coach of Christ to teach and tell

Bringing those to heaven's gate

Get busy; come on, before it's too late!

This is not the time to debate

This is not the time to wait

Of your inhibition toss

Before more people are lost

We don't have to do it on our own

For his seeds are already sown

But if you do your part

He will work within their heart

Jeremiah 8:20

Joel 3:13

Matthew 9:37-38

The Calling

The fog surrounds us like a ghost in the night
At the sound of a horn birds scatter in fright
The mist so thick it leaves moistened tear
This insecure feeling, prickling my hair

What has made this feeling?
come on so strong?
Someone is kneeling
something is wrong

Then through the garden
I see them emerge
Peter grabs his sword
and takes off an ear
He takes it in his hand
and puts it back in place

He goes with them easy
it's time for his flight
Even though he knows
He can call on the Father
He'd come in His might
But He knows of His calling
and what He must do
This is the following
That He must go through
To die for us so we can
make it to skies so blue
This is his calling
This He is willing to do . . .

Luke 22:39-46

Winter Whisper

The wind blows north to south

leaves dance a melancholy song

Whispers dark winter coming

snow is felt winter whispers

A bone chill but yet

season harvest lingers to toil

A hope to gather a remnant

for souls should not perish

Jeremiah 8:20

John 4:35

The Fawn

I looked at her

Elegant and tall

Biggest brown eyes I ever saw

She stopped to look

Stretching my hand to her

Come here baby girl

Can I touch your fur?

She twitched her ear

Not sure what to do

We exchange unspoken respect

She moved just a little

Before she took off and flew

Psalm 42:1

Whisper a Prayer

In the quiet of the morning

I whisper a prayer

Praying through the day

That you will be there

Hope for the day to go

Just as planned

Knowing it will be better

If you hold my hand

I've learned that the days

Can hold all kind of strife

But whatever is to come

It is better with you in my life.

Psalm 55:17

Matthew 26:41

Philippians 4:6

Behind The Sunset

Where children play run and laugh

Breeze whips through memories past

Songs of life tickling the air

Life was sung without a care

True love danced a favorite song

Tipping, swaying, singing along

Tides rushed in, to and fro

Oh this life so long to go

Sunsets go but never last

Days go by oh so fast

Memories play of life's rich song

Where has all the sunsets gone

Isaiah 60:20

Sun Painting

Sun Painting on the water
my mood it reflects
ever changing images
my mind to collect

The colors come and they go
a first hint of gray
breaks the black of the night
yet bit of the day

With morning light
A soft purple gives way
to some gold
to wondering the day

then changing to blue
an ever changing scene
for my changing mood
Oh, the thoughts,

flash through my mind
these colors you give
all the colors of life
I see your artistry
in the morning light

I see your hand
in the darkest night . . .

Ecclesiastes 11:7
Matthew 5:45

342

Autumn

Spread for me a crimson path

Before does come the winter's wrath

So I might feel like a princess of royalty

Paint for me tis your gift of specialty

Friends with wings sing to you gather

For the trip to endless summer weather

I might have a glimpse of splendor

Till Heaven's Gate I do render

Psalm 15:11

Early Morning

I need to sleep

I feel your breath

It whispers in my ear

Come into me

I reach my hands to heaven

You hug me in my sleepy

With a reassuring smile

It invites me to open

All the heavy gates

Let me lay them before you

Aw but I came to thank you

Not to ask you

You again smile

And I feel you say

I know . . . .

Psalm 63:1

Shawn's Poem

Little Blue blanket

Snug and warm

Tumbling bears

Riding motor bikes n' cars

Little hands, five-fingers,

Perfect toes

All set in place

A cute little nose

You my son,

Such a blessing to me

I am so proud

I want all to see

A grown man now

With a wife and child

Tall Handsome and strong

With heart lovingly mild

Proverbs 23:26

Psalm 113:9

The House on the Hill

Trees that sway reflect from the broken glass window

A flash from the approaching electrical storm is the only light seen from its pane.

The torn curtain looks like a human disfigured and old . . .

Watching for the uninvited guest

The old black Iron Gate makes for a nervous moan.

It sways with the wind squeaking back and forward

In the distance a wolf cry's as the moon is covered by a dark cloud.

The grandness of the old house is seen from afar

Abandoned Empty from the wane of wealth

Inside the only residents crawl around the rooms

Sneaking from the cracked corners to fly in the night

Seeking out food for yet another generation of their own

Soon the weathered wood will rot and fall

Leaving a mere pile of refuge

Far too gone to reconstruct

Like a depression of worthless sense

The stories of children tales

Ring to its glory

Of phantoms and ghouls

And other most mystical of creatures

But is it just an old house

It's owner gone on

Left unattended to its own

Waiting . . . Waiting . . . Waiting . . .

Lamentations 2:7

Romans 8:23

346

He Came To Take You Back

He came to take you back

Slithering from the ground

Morphing into beauty

With a covert ghastly fate

He knows his limited time

He anticipates the favorable

He must whisper to you

He snickers at his wait

The time must be right

Weakened you must be

By all that surrounds

The right time to bait

Listen can you hear him snarl

He can't keep it intact

His eyes are seeping evil

He came to take you back

Luke 22:31

Painting the Sunrise

Whispering Heart paint me a sunrise

Brush it with yellows and gold

As sun kisses the morning

brush awakens the canvas

with colors beautiful and bold!

Psalm 84:11-12

Stumbled

I stumble at anticipations door

Where the passionate sun illuminates light

The darkest cloud fell to the earth hindering my travel

The misty moon afar fogs my human eye

But lo, the vision door is closed like dead of night

Latched in place no longer waiting my hand

Wishes dances under the midnight sky

Wave through this soul,

dreams are still fresh in babbling heart

Where might I find such kindred spirit?

Who speaks this language as I?

For his wings flap not with me to sing

I was too late,

on he went to sing another song . . .

Proverbs 3:23

Night of Dreams

I open my world in twilight sky

By the light of the midnight sand

Dream a great prince to take my tired hand

We journey to the land of dreams

Where snowflakes taste like honey

sip from a river made of sweet mint tea

talk of summer days, playing in the sun

where we leave footprints of golden hue

We'll stay together until morning dawn

sends the angels to light the eastern sky

Wishing to stop the clock, not whisper a goodbye

Yet, he must flutter off, on lighted wings

He sings enchanted farewell songs

My heart will wither as he fades

With the sun kissed morning dew

Dreams can only last, until the night is through

Genesis 32:28

CHAPTER 11

Walking the Sonlit Path

Let me walk in the light

That I might feel heaven

Let the light shine in warmth

Let my face radiate of you

That I might be blind to me

Let the water ripples my steps

That you may be felt in the oceans

Reflective of your divine heart

Let the skies only see ahead

Not too far back as I've stumbled

I was learning to walk the path

Clouds sometime shadow my way

Let me hold your hand in the dark

That I might find my way back out

But now as the sun brightens

Let me be filled with your light

Psalm 16:11

Breakfast Morning Out

Her hair of blond curls,
hang in her face.
She looks at her food,
in a joyful mood.

She swipes at her hair,
with jellied fingers . . .
Breakfast morning,
Her favorite trip . . .

Big Blue eyes
look up at you,
as of her milk
she takes a sip . . .

She rolls her eyes,
at your coffee.
Everything on her plate
in her syrup goes for a dip . . .

She spies a crayon
by her plate . . .
Stuffs it in her pocket
for a later date . . .

Breakfast morning
is almost done.
Her next adventure
For her to run . . .

She takes off
in her blinking shoes . . .
Leaving you,
to pay what's due . . .

Psalm 103:17

Dawn the Day

Bare canvas awaits a brush stroke

dawn starts to paint the eastern sky

flowers have all been kissed with dew

Tom cat winding his body around my ankle

Hoping to be fed his dish of tuna

A sigh escapes from resigned lips

I whisper a prayer from my heart

I'll do His will, He does His part

Then I yawn and yawn again

The liquid help not yet seeped

But the day is ready to begin

Proverbs 27:1

Beyond The Sun

The empty tire swings
With the winds wings
The laughter of days gone by
The sound a wind whistle sighs

Wheat fields sweep
In a timeless beat
In my mind to host
A forlorn melancholy ghost

A distant dog barks
The call of flying larks
Brings me back to check
To this heart it becks

I smile feeding the birds
Who wait with chirping words?
For me to walk away
They care not for me to stay

I lean back in my tattered chair
Watching scenes play through the air
A stage of theater plays in the sky
As each gray cloud passes by

Have I drifted in sleep?
I see an angel peep
From way up on high
Swooping down as he goes by

He takes me by the hand
Leading to another land
To adventures I must run
To a far off home beyond the sun

Hebrews 8:13
Revelation 21:4
Ephesians 2:6

I Miss You

I miss you

Tears fall like water falls

It is so lonely

I hate this world

I hate this thing called death

My head is in pain

But not as much as my heart

Oceans drop on my chest

I need a hug

But none to be found

Not just any hug

Your hug

The tight bear hug

That was yours alone

No one around

I hit the wall in pain

My hand swells

But I can't feel

I scream your name

You're not coming back

Why are you on the other side?

Too soon, Too soon

I miss you

Revelation 21:4

Demon Dark

Demon dark, I won't let you come in!

Demon dark, You know you won't win

You try to take away my smile

You fill me up with such bile

You slap me hard, and then you run

You try to take away my Sun

You bring with you dark clouds of doom

That kind of thinking takes one to tomb

You bring this enviable doubt

All I want is to lay and pout

I lift my eyes to say a prayer

it helps to bear my burdens there

Christ long ago won this fight

Demons of dark take your flight

Lamentations 3:6-26

The Armor

When the trials get heavy
And the road seems low
There are some things
I think you should know

This is a test
A school if you would
To see what our use will be
In another neighborhood

One with no bounds
No dips in the road
One where we will help
Someone else with their load

Oh the perks
With an Armor of Light
With a Sword of His Spirit
Feet shod in the gospel of right

With faith we have His shield
To wear a waistband of truth
A helmet of His salvation yield
To breastplate of His righteousness!

Ephesians 6:10-17

Fantasy World

She lives in a fantasy world

where pain is forbidden.

Here to fight evil with good.

Where everything ends as it should.

Here the fights always lost by the villain!

Scenes how they play like a TV show,

She plays the drama director

She puts on her suit complete with a cape.

Calls her trusted companion

Off to solve the next case,

to save the human race.

Down life's deepest canyon

but it's only an escape

from the pain that's kept hidden.

In a mystical fantasy world

Where reality is forbidden

Psalm 126:1

Broken

I am in this despair Lord

I feel overwhelmed

I feel helpless to pull myself up

I need A touch

I need your help

Guide my faltering step

Help me focus

I need to feel loved

I feel unworthy

I ask for help

Take this battle

Arm me with your power

I don't have on my own

I feel so weak torn down

I won't make it without you

I will surely die

2 Chronicles 20:15

Not Too Far Away

Enchanting rays dance with glistering sunshine
Dewdrops shine as diamonds sparkle
Green grass sways, wind gives the rhythm
Lightning flashes from the distant hill

The storm moves in chasing away the sun
The rain sprinkles misty damp
The tears join as I think of you
Miles away in another land

No green meadows only dry sand
No rain to dance with the dew
My heart pounds as the thunder wails
Trampling the grass like a rail train

I'm missing you, feel my pain
Arms would have held me tight
In the storm and through the night
I wrap myself in my own arms

Pretend you are in this room
A soft melody whispers our tune
I dance and sway in your arms
A star falls from the sky

We wish together from different lands
Dream together enchanted muse
I'm not really alone I feel you
Your hand in mine,

Means the rest of you,
Is not too far away . . .

Matthew 28:20

Rain Out Of My Window

Rain out my window
Sliding down the pane
Drops running down
Making me go insane

I couldn't see why
You had to leave me?
To remedy this feeling
I enter a fantasy world.

It takes me spinning.
In adventures on the Sea,
Oh the times you would
Come along with me . . .

The winds and rain
Would toss our tiny ship
We didn't care, as long
As we had this time to share . . .

I return to reality . . .
I step into the rain,
The cold it matches
My broken heart . . .

The rain mixes with
My tears of pain . . .

Psalm 34:17-19

Forever Yours

I will dance with you till morning light

We will dance away the night

I will look into your eyes so kind

I'll see the stars that reflect from mine

We will walk where your garden grows

Whispering secrets only God knows

I will tell you of my love so true

You will embrace me to say you love me too

The last star fades to end the night

The sky turns to dawns first light

You will ask to be my only one

I will be yours until life on earth is done

Psalm 113:7-9

Songs of Solomon 5:16

A Refreshing Fountain

I sing to you my love

With you here by my side

I know in my heart

You'll always be my guide

Some think you set

On a throne high in the sky

Yet I know in my heart

You are always close by

Life's road may travel through

Deep valleys and high mountains

Yet you are there with me

Like a refreshing fountain

Bringing water when I thirst

Filling me with love to burst

Isaiah 35:7

The Fight

I did everything, to push you away

you did everything, for you could stay

I rained down on your party

your love for me was still hardy

I laughed and made fun, like your life was a game

I talked behind your back forgetting your name

I told you to get out of my life, I wanted to be free!

You turned to my face, Saying, "You still loved me" . . .

You pull me into your embrace

In your arms I buried my face

I should have loved you all the time

How could I have been that blind!

I love you Lord . . .

Jeremiah 8:5

Jeremiah 31:3

Amber's Poem

Wrapped snug
In a pink fluffy blanket
They handed you to me
Eyes already open
The world you wanted to see

Little hands,
Five-fingers,
Perfect toes
All set in place
A cute little nose

Curly golden hair
Eyes like the sky
Giggles that rock heaven
As you wander by

You my Daughter
Such a blessing to me
I am so proud
Of what you've grown to be

A lovely strong woman
A heart pure as gold
With true hearted convictions
Wonderfully bold

2 Corinthians 6:18

What Does It Take

What does it take?

To see a heart break

The feeling gone

Like an old love song

Someone did someone wrong?

What does it take?

To start living, like new?

Get the head out the pillow

Getting back to old you?

Can that person come back?

Has it all been changed?

With a mended heart

But now rearranged?

Hosea 6:1

Ezekiel 11:19

Oh This Feeling, It's So Fine

I feel so full of his love sometime

He is just so very sublime

I know he has blessed me so

I feel his love from my head to my toe

I only wish you all could feel

His love that is so very real

It is free! If you just ask

Please don't make it a hard task

He said just believe in me

I will then set you free

Oh this feeling, it's so fine

Nothing better, of any kind

Make Jesus, Your Lord today

Ask Him in your Heart to stay

Songs of Solomon 5

The Legacy

The pain you have endured

More than anyone should at

A tender learning age

I hope you grow strong and healthy

My prayer for you is peace faith and love

Understanding, it may not come in this life,

But remember it is for a higher reason

Be bold and tender kind and accomplished

Learn with a vengeance to make you proud

But be not arrogant, for all to see your work

As honorable and noble, don't be too proud,

Listen, mistakes are steps in learning

Be not hindered by them, but learn and prosper

Honor those in authority,

But remember they too are but human.

Colossians 3:16

The Music

The music begins with a
soft almost inaudible sound.
Soft as the breath of a baby
even and almost a whisper

Building to a quiet
but steady pump, pump
the sound goes on,
like a heart in pulse.

My spirit is lifted
to that of a bird on a perch
at the top of the nest . . .

The music takes a melody
swaying to and fro.
Like sailing a gentle sea
then with a buildup
of the sounds

My soul is lifted
I slight from this perch
wings are spread.

The wind adds a push!

Soaring to the music

with these imagined wings

Lost in the spirit of it all

I see a door that is open.

The music takes me

spiraling forward.

A magnificent pace!

The light from the door illuminates

so that it is round about me,

but far still.

The music has brought me here

in spirit.

The Joy, Kinship, Love.

Beyond words of this world!

For this time, just a visit.

But someday for all time!

Lamentations 3:63

Love All

It's easy to love them that love you,
It's easy to love,
The cute, not the blue.

We see a tear,
It's hard to bear.
What can we do?
Turn head or stare?

It's easy to love
Them that are kind.
The message from above
Says love them that whine.

Those that are mean
It's quite harder though.
But that's the message,
Sent here below.

Trying your passions
Or building a bridge.
It's all relations
Out on this ridge.

Love all mankind,
Matters not how they act.
This you will find,
Is the Godly track.

Matthew 5:44-46

A Bed to Sleep

Sweep the floor

Mop the floor

Cook the food

Wash the dishes

Wash the clothes

Fold the clothes

Bath the cat

Dust the tables

Make the bed

Vacuum the floor

Make the lunches

Pay the bills

Write the checks

Balance the check book

Get the mail

A bed to make

Thank you Lord

I have

Loved ones to love

A floor to sweep

A floor to mop

Food to cook

Dishes to wash

Clothes to wash

Clothes to fold

Tables to dust

A bed to make

A vacuum to use

Family to share

Money for bills

An income to survive

A checkbook to balance

My own address

A house to live in

An income to balance

A bed to sleep . . .

Psalm 95

Thanksgiving the Unexpected Visitor

The cats are under my feet, I am working on dinner.

We have two, Samantha and Tommy.

I have had enough! Out they go!

After dinner, I thought I'd give them

a little leftover turkey I put it in a bowl

I was intending to put it on the front porch.

A few hours later I let them in the back door.

I go to get the bowl from the front.

There is the visitor eating from the bowl

Two feet from our front door . . .

He looks up at me with big black eyes.

A sleek black coat, with a white streak down his back!

He looks up at me unafraid,

I slowly back into the house!

I watch from the window, he has his fill.

Then looks back at me and waddles away!

Full from my Turkey,

On Thanksgiving Day!

2 Corinthians 9:15

TV Oppression

I listen to the TV
What do I see?

Looks like another
Awful crime spree

It's how the stories unfold
Doctor Steals from the old

Desperate people rob bank
The announcers musing ranks

Come on over to see the bloom of spring
It's the garden show of the life time!

All for the great price of
Twenty dollars at the door

Boyfriend takes hostage then kills himself
All for the seeking of wealth

While loading the gun, He meant no harm
Man dies on grate while trying to keep warm.

Come on over to our fine diner to eat

It's a great value at fifty dollars a seat!

Man reaches for her left hand
Diamonds are a girl's best friend

We wonder why we're so mixed up
All this in half an hour

Even superman
Jumps off the water tower

Stock markets fall
Food prices are high

Can of soup, buck twenty five
How can the poor stay alive?

It's just ninety nine dollars
A month for this wonderful invention

Now we have to buy some sort of extension
Or we will lose this wonderful connection . . .

Psalm 42:9

Psalm 107:39

Ecclesiastes 7:7

Faith of the Mustard Seed

Transform me that I believe
You'll take care of every need

If I just have the faith
The size of a mustard seed
Matthew 17:20

After all you are the one
Who on water walked?
Matthew 14:26

You're the only one
That could make a donkey talk
Numbers 22:29

You opened eyes with mud
For someone that was blind
John 9:14

For a man that was mad
You sent the madness into swine
Matthew 8:33

Surely I can believe
You'll take care of all my need

Help me have the faith
In your loving plan

Even though sometimes it's hard
For this mere mortal to understand

2 Timothy 2:7

His Love

She seen the light of him standing there
But thought, for me Christ could not care
I mess this life up all the time
He's here for someone more sublime

But his hand was outstretched
She felt like she was such a wretch
She turns to see if someone else was there
It couldn't be for her He'd care

As soon as his hand touched her skin
She became aware of all her sin
The sobs escaped from somewhere in her heart
It's OK; I'll take them, sin now part

She watched as blood like sweat ran from his face
She knew then He'd died to save her a place
Someday I'll take you home with me
But there are still those who need set free

With that message, He was gone
She knew then she must continue on
To share the love she'd found that day
So for on earth now she would stay

Romans 8:39

Reflection of a Dream

I set alone
me and my thoughts.
Dreams of this moment
over shadow ought.

The sand at my feet
is warm between my toes.
Where this dream will
take, nobody knows.

A glimpse of the Sunrise
Reflects on the ocean
Water splashing,
the only motion

A Seagull, sweeps by,
In search of a fish.
Life always this peaceful
Is only a wish.

Soon all will be awake
Ready for the day.
Give me a little
more time to dream.
This special time away . . .

Job 20:8

What a Day

What a day, what can I say

It started out bad when I put my head out the door

My cat had puked all over the garage floor

I spent 4 hours writing an eccentric write

Only to come back to my PC to find it had took flight

My mind began to race

But no use it was lost in cyberspace

I wrote an EBay auction

but my camera was a lost concoction

After doing all the description

I had to terminate the expedition

I decide to take a nap

I rested my hands in my lap

Then I remember what I forgot that day

I bowed my head to take the time to pray

Psalm 137:1

John 14:26

My Rock

In the quiet how can I feel alone?

The darkness depth about the room

The numbers shine from the clock

My mind reaches out for you my rock

You are here with me, I am not alone

I feel you through my every bone

I know you have much to do,

Please hear my call until I'm through

I think this is what I'm supposed to do

As through the tears I call for you

The list goes on for help abound

But strength in you is always found . . .

You are more than a name to know

Though you help my tour below

Let me praise you by the tree

The one where you died for me

2 Samuel 22:2-4

My Rock

No silêncio como posso sentir sozinho

a profundidade trevas sobre a sala

os números do relógio brilhar

Minha mente estende a mão para você a minha rocha

Você está aqui comigo, eu não estou sozinho

Eu sinto que você através de todos os meus ossos

Eu sei que você tem muito a ver,

Por favor, ouça meu chamado, até que eu sou meio

Eu acho que isso é o que eu devo fazer

Como através das lágrimas que eu chamo por você

A lista continua para ajudar abundam

Mas a força em você é sempre encontrado.

Está mais do que um nome para conhecer

Apesar de você ajudar a minha turnê abaixo

Deixe-me te louvo pela árvore

Aquele em que você morreu por mim

Adoring Love

I bow my head humbled
You are my God, always have been
I need to feel your touch each day
I want to walk in your light
Guided by your arms about me

Tears fall down my cheek
You are here, I feel you
In the breeze, that ruffles my hair
The sun kiss on my shoulder

The storm that whirls about
You are ominous
You rule, but let me choose
Hold my hand when I am weak

Help me to please you
For I know it is best
Contentment only you can bring
I enjoy this world you gave

Yet, I know it is not all it could be
I marvel at that thought
We have invited darkness, yet
Oh, the promises of a new earth

I look at the glory of heavens

Far beyond my human eye

I see the care that each bee

Gives free to the flower

The love you have bestowed to me

Gentle, caring like new love coupled

Your love is in the new mother's eye

I rejoice in your endlessly gifts

Come walk it my garden

Touch me with dew kisses

Scented by rose petals

Hinted with lilac breeze

I treasure your gifts, savor the love

I stand on tiptoes, hands stretched

Reaching, moved triumph,

Enclosed by adoring love

Psalm 71:14

CHAPTER 12

Broken Wings

Your wings will heal,

You'll fly again,

too far off places,

You've never been,

Oh what adventure!

You will see!

Be my friend,

fly with me!!

Malachi 4:2

Enchanted Angels Sing

Whisper butterfly in my ear
Tell me the word I want to hear

Take me on your velvet wings
Where all the enchanted angels sing

Take me to this far off light
Beyond my dreaming in the night

Hold me upon the mountain peak
Where words aren't needed to speak

I'll be yours till endless day
When all we know falls away

Then you'll take me by my hand
Bringing me to another land

Full of so much more to learn
Much more than I've ever earned

My heart swells at thy thought
All your life on earth has bought

Luke 2:13-14

Sometimes My Halo Tilts a Bit

Sometimes my halo tilts a bit

That's when you reach down and straighten it

I know all the right things to do

But the earthly trials, I go through!

They take me on a trip you see

Making me what I shouldn't be

They slide in my mind like ice

The picture, isn't always nice

Lord I'm glad you don't give up on me

You put my halo in the place it should be

Like a father to his child

When he gets out of sort, and little wild

Reaching down that great big hand

Take a hold of my mine, where I stand

Lead me in my journey here

So someday, I'll make it there

Romans 7:18-25

The Flight of the Snowflake

When I fall to the ground I hope to be . . .

Something Regal, for all to see . . .

My hope is for hands to mold . . .

Something tall and bold . . .

Maybe I'll stand six feet tall!

Joined with others roll in a ball . . .

I'll have a mouth and nose.

I even hope for fancy clothes . . .

No matter what I want to bring joy.

It's the hope for every snowflake boy.

Since the tales, of snowman Frosty.

It's the dream for every snowflake,

This wonderful life to make . . .

Isaiah 45:7-9

Lord Will See Me Through

All to soon taken away
To a land where angels play
Touching our life with joyful flutter
You'll be missed like no other

Walking shores with sands of gold
Oh the stories, I'll be told
Wishing I could be with you
In that land so dear and true

Someday again your smile I'll see
I'll miss you till that day with thee
But now I must tarry on here
Until the Lord calls me dear

I pray the Lord will see me through
Until my time of calling is due
Sometimes it's hard to understand
But know the Lord has an ultimate plan

But Lord touch us left behind
With your hand, loving and kind
The heart so raw, left to bleed
Give us your shoulder, when in need.

Psalm 23:6

Wars of Realms

A demon fell hard as he was knocked down by angel wings
The earth quaked from its center
They rattle still as they tumbled and roll in fight
Knocking each other to and fro

The toll was high and the battle a long way from being over
But the war must not stop the loss would mean the loss of man
A demon blew hard sure to destroy the earth tornadoes were formed
But the angels kept them from destroying the whole of the world

Wondering on sadden by the people lost.
But ready to meet the faithful one's to take them to a heavenly home
Only if more would pray
It would ignite strength for the angel's to complete their task

God tells the angel's keep going
There are still some that have not heard of me
Everyone must have a chance to know me
They must all know before the end and victory

A demon sends a freeze through the land
Disables the town so no one can come together for fellowship
Gods sends a message to the hearts
On the tip of angel wings

Revelation Chapters 7-9

Dried Roses

Roses dry and pedals fall

Stems die on thorn pricks tall

Scent lingers in the light

Breezing on through the night

Oh, fragrant rose on the wind

Whispering rapture around to send

Quilts fazing like the moon

Lingering in a blissful tune

Calling to a mindful song

Oh this feeling can't be wrong

Mysteries play its fluted note

Singing again the song she wrote

Songs of Solomon 2:1

Note to God

Only you do I see

you reflect in my being

give me love

beyond my world

I am old worn used

you give youth

hope usefulness

I only hope

I can be worthy

Colossians 1:9-16

Recycle

Wastes not want not
Some just don't have a lot
There I am curb side shopping
Or maybe garage sale hopping

It is some ones junk might be to treasure
It's all things I love to measure
I like to see what something else might be
I said this before; it's the artist in me

You might take a tattered blanket
With saved buttons and remake it
Into a cuddly Bear
For someone you care

A piece of wood cut so fine
Can read your favorite fun line
A leaking bucket, fill with flowers
I could go on for hours

Just, recycle, reuse
Save a little Earth
In the renew.

Matthew 6:21

I Need You Near

Hold me in your arms when I fear

Show me you are near

You wipe away my tears

Take on your shoulders my cares

I try to be brave, but I fall

Yet for you I want to stand tall

You pick me up, brush me off

You heal me when I have a cough

Without you I am nothing

But in you, I'll always be something

Isaiah 41:10

Heart Yearn

When grass turns from green to brown,

touched with white frost tips.

When the warm breeze

coming from South.

Changes to a northern flow

with bits of snow.

When the warm air

turns a bitter blow.

My heart yearns, for the warm heart

Of Spring to show.

Psalm 84:2

Gift of Snow

Lone flake floating
from the sky
I watch in wonder
as you go by

Another, I know
will follow soon
with lots to
fall by noon

Oh the enchantment
that you bring
the Joys of
winter you do sing

You bring in the
Christmas season
with each snowflake
Jesus is the reason

A babe in a manger
Is what will ring
all through the night
the Angels Sing.

All through the heavens
about peace on earth
brought by Gods child
His miracle birth!

Job 38:22
Psalm 51:7
Romans 5:15-18

The Vessel

What can this vessel do?
you to fill me to the top
that I might bring water
to the soul that thirst

Hope to the one
that needs strength
only by you
these things can I do

I am willing,
please use me
anoint, lead, guide.
Faith seen, faith learned

Touching a heart,
that hearts be touched
not for me to be seen,
but through me, seeing you

For I am the vessel
You are God!
Acts 9:15
Romans 9:21

I Hear Music

I feel safe in my home here
it is warm comfortable mmm.
I don't know how I got here
I feel snug, protected.

I don't have a name yet
but, "Hope" is nice.
I don't know how but
there is knowledge.

This is not a permanent place
but a place to grow and learn.
No one knows of me yet.
How excited they will be!

I hear infiltrating music
singing me to slumber
with soft whispering lullabies
I snuggle in warm comfort

I just heard them talk!

They know me now.

They didn't sound excited

maybe angry is a better word.

What is that it's making me dizzy!

Oh! What an awful feeling!

Please stop, don't do that to me!

Oh! Oh! I'm spinning, my head!

What is that rattling my chest?

Very hard and cold, pulling

It is hard for me to hold on

But I cling tight!

The noise deafens my cries

My eyes flutter at first light

No I can't leave this place!

It is too early!

Please! Please! Stop!

Psalm 127:3

Jeremiah 1:5

Alien under the Christmas tree

The Little girl eyed the presents
Like a porcelain vintage doll
Covered in lace and velvet
Leaving everyone in Awe

Hoping to see a peek
Of a gift hid in the paper
Under the green leaves
Of Tree of mass taper

Some tiny movement took her back
For a much closer inspection
Under the biggest covered box
A blue eye blinked in her direction

Her little eyes turned to saucers
As the gift that peered at her
Made another movement
That made her eyes a blur

Should she scream for mama
Or take another look
She had not seen the likes
In any of her books!

But somewhere in her mind
She knew he was of no harm
Something inside of her
Knew he was a charm

She scampered to the candy dish
To find them both a treat
She thought that if she fed him
Her he would not eat!

She filled her little velvet purse
Full as it could be
then looked for a place
To hide beneath the tree

She found a little opening
Way back in the back
Between a little box
and a great big sack

In hope that he would find her
She snuggled in for a little rest
Soft moans of munching candy
Coming from her chest

Soon she seen him moving
Around the great big sack
She put her hand up to her mouth
To keep a scream intact!

He blinked his big blue eyes
Taking her all in
Wondering if there was a fight
Did he have a chance to win!

But he seen her smile
Tugging at her lips
The little peace offering
In her finger tips

He was so hungry
Had not eaten in days
He reached out for her offering
Not knowing of her ways

He brought the red jelly
To his nose to have a sniff
It smelled strange to him
He took another whiff

Before he knew what happened
He plopped it between his lips
To his delight he liked it
He licked his finger tips

He looked to the small doll
Underneath a decked out tree
He knew he had the greatest gift
That there could ever be . . . .

1 Corinthians 13:13

Guardian Angel

Will you protect me?
Will you hold me tight?
Will you fight the fight
I cannot see?
Will you always be with me?

Let me know I'm not alone.
That I'm not here on my own.

It's too dark do you see.
The casting shadows
around that tree!

Won't you make a little light?
To let me know it's alright.

I know you must hide from my sight.
For if I see you death be my plight.

But Guardian Angel all my own
Please don't leave me all alone.

Guardian Angel
Please don't sleep.
You have a promise to keep . . .

1 Corinthians 6:3
Psalm 91:11

Deep

Oh the dream flowing

Flowing deep in wonders

Wonders that touch the heart

Heart that beats to your muse

Muse that walks in our dreams

Dreams that whisper love

Love beyond the understanding

Understanding not the mystery

Mystery that surrounds us to feel

Feel the heart deep touching

Touching our together

Together in a dream

Dream to the core

Core of our breathe

Breathe to our life

Life of dreams

Beside the muse

Muse of dreams

John 14:18

A Note from God

Are you thirsty?
then drink,
but nothing shall quench
the dry of your mouth

Are you hungry?
your plate is high with the feast of this world,
the bounty of your hand has much
but you are not full

You work hard to make a living
your castle is full with riches of that labor
you want for nothing
yet you are not content

Your house is full
with children of your body all around
they look only at your worth
yet you feel not loved

You have earned all this
but until you know me
you will not have peace
you thirst for my word

Hungry for my presence
empty without my love
your home will mean little without My Spirit,
God.

Proverbs 1:2-3

Saint Nicholas

Green tree, golden tinsel

Round red bulbs, berry garland

White snowmen, Crochet snowflakes

silver bell, glitter shapes

bright star at the highest peak

mini village looking all too real,

lays lit at your feet.

All decked out in radiant splendor.

Awaits A visitor from a fantasy world.

White hair long white beard

chubby chap, pinked cheeks

dress in royalty fare.

Red velvet with white fur trim.

Given to keep warm, by the polar bear!

Catered to by little people with pointed ears

Very devoted don't have a fear!

This all brings you gifts of cheer.

The hope that Saint Nicholas is near . . .

Proverbs 19:6

Isaiah 1:23

Ecclesiastes 5:19

A Poem for Misty

She's a beautiful young lady

inside and out.

She gives more love than anyone

scurrying about

She has a hug for all

where she sees a tear.

She may never be a leader.

or even own her own home

She's one of God's special gifts

that he has sent our way

With her loving innocent smile,

to brighten up our day

Jeremiah 1:5

Proverbs 15:15

Together

I lean lightly to kiss your brow

Thinking and wondering, oh how,

How did I get so very blessed?

When I won you from all the rest

Hair that heaven kissed with gold

Arms strong for you to hold

Tight . . . to the love we jointly share

Words of love we whisper in care

Dinner shared by candle light

Is romantic true and quite polite

Hot dogs thick with special sauce

A shared movie by a coin toss

Simply everyday waking by your side

In this life of a carousel ride

Up and down and round and round

Standing side by side in all that's found

Songs of Solomon 5:16

The First Christmas

The ground sparkles like diamonds
Starlight spreads through the land
The aurora sings with high energy
Something is about to happen my friend

The goats are too quiet, the lambs do not bawl
Something has happened to put them in awe!
I see many around a stable, what's happened in there?
Many persons stand at the door, trying to stare!

The city is bustling, one can hardly move
No place for another, no place to groove
Many have made the long traveling route
They came from all over for the census count

The murmurs grow spreading through the crowd
A baby is born. God blessed them abound
Not just a baby, is what I have heard
A king in the stable, that is absurd!

It is written in the scripture they say
It's tells us all of this coming day!!
A Savior to be born, yet the highest king
The heavenly host, His story gloriously sings!

Isaiah 9:6-7
Luke 2:11-12

Why Is That Tune Stuck In My Head?

The cookies are done all snug in their jar
The tree is all decorated topped with a star

The bank accounts empty, even the reserve
The tree skirt covered with things not deserved

Away in the manger, no crib for a bed
Why is that tune stuck in my head?

Holiday movies glare from the screen
The most active adventure I've ever seen!

The parties all scheduled written in my book
The only one I open to have a look

Away in the manger, no crib for a bed
Why is that tune stuck in my head?

Looks like everything is set in place
I have a feeling some things been misplaced

Just like Santa I check my list twice
Everything done everything nice

Away in the manger, no crib for a bed
Why is that tune stuck in my head?

Matthew 6:33

Mary's Story

I've never known a man . . .
Yet here I am with child
by God's call.

My betroth Joseph
could have sent me away . . .

But an angel came to him
told him to stay . . .

We were married.
Now we must travel to Bethlehem

our taxes to pay . . .
Everywhere we look is full

no place for us to stay.
The baby I carry

is ready to be born.
Faith that I have

let's me know
it will be OK . . .

Luke 1:26-35

Child, Oh Child

Child, Oh Child
Born of above

Watched over by Angels
Sent with pure love

Sent to mere humans
Trusted in their care

A Savior to all
The burdens to bear

Born to such meager
Life here below

In heaven of royalty
Men you must woe

Some learned to love you
Some turned you away

All will know you
On judgment day

Isaiah 9:6-7

Molding Vessels

Some are simple

Some are round

Some are thin

Some are bound

With plants and soil

Sand and cactus

Turn us around

On your atlas

Mold us with your loving hand

Blending with the earthly sands

Turning us on the grinding stone

Boldly bring us to your own

Use this vessel as you see fit

Fill us with your heavenly wit

Make our clay something of worth

Something of good to use on earth

Isaiah 45:9

Isaiah 64:8

But Never My Word

The old earth groans with age
Prediction cries to be unleashed
God holds back with His hand
Calamity barks to be loosed

God remembers his promise
That all might hear of His grace
He calls those to his work
It is hard to find willing vessels

But like scripture foretold
There is some that answer
The work changes lives
It is all done for love

Holding the aged earth together
While building a new place
Puts a smile on his face
Sadness because more won't come

Can you feel the strain
The white horse nasals flares
The angel draws a sword
God's voice says not yet

Soon I will mount and claim
Them to me that know me
Then the earth shall have her own
Heaven and Earth shall pass
But never my word

Matthew 5:18

Wishing To Meet You

Sometimes I get discouraged

I think you're so far away,

I wish I could reach up to meet you,

Could you put your hand my way?

I wish there was an entrance

A way to come and go . . .

But I know that's not the way life works.

I have to wait down here below . . .

1 Thessalonians 4:17

Burnt Out

Sometimes I just feel burnt out

What is that all about?

The pain

The gain

The willful game

The company

It all seems the same

Down on life

Sex and love

Whatever happened to

God above?

Please don't give me any thought

I am rambling of what I ought!!

Psalm 19:14

Discouraged

I sat here cold,

Feeling so dumb!

My mind is blank,

I just feel numb!

What was I thinking?

When I thought,

I could write a book!

I didn't think of all it took!

But I will just keep

Writing, as I feel . . .

Maybe someday,

It will be real . . .

Galatians 6:9

Isaiah 40:29

The Last Page

I remember sauntering to the stars

Wishing to have a glance at the moon

The sea rolled in and out laughing,

Leaving the fossils of enchanted urchins

We would have the best night ride

On the mist maid of dreams ray

Touching and magically enchanting

A mystery beyond the philosophy

Yet the night walks now a dark path

The wrath of empty has reached shore

Who is to blame, the story merely ended

It is sad to close the last page of a book

The Last Book . . . Revelation 20:12

Chapter 1

Happy New Year
Busting Butt
Hooked
Chains
Growing Prayer
The Quest
Prisoner of Snow
Trying out my new snow shoes
Touch me in the Morning
Winter Dreams
The Last War, Armageddon
I am Leaving
God's Love
Deceiving Sun
The Trail of Ice Queens
If the Moon Failed to Shine
My Lovers
Winter Wonderland
Faithful Morning
Flavored Ice Cream
It Wasn't a Dream
The Rush
Black Feather
Winter's Claim
I Let You Fly
Cold Weather
Made By God
Snow Globe by God
Thy Gift
The Dowry
Howling Lone

Chapter 2

While You're Sleeping

Shan't Care

People Need You Lord

Before The Rooster Cry

Leftovers

Gift of Rhyme

Snowed In

Moon Set

Letting Go

Through The Door

Looking Silly

Cupid's Arrow

Chocolate Dreams

Be Mine

His Love

The Morning

Until Next Time We Meet

Should I Not Be Jealous

Seasons

Now I Can't Go

Wondering

Shelter in a Storm

This Unimportant Human Girl

Dreams of Tomorrow

The Kiss

Twinkle In My Eyes

Love Kissed Muse

How Much Do You Love Me

Leap Day Quest

Chapter 3

Chapter 4

In The Way

Tempting Walk

The Unicorn

The Fallen Empire

God's Son

A Walk to Paradise

Jesus Asks "Why?"

Risen Savior

The Quest of a Bunny

PC Blues

Angel Fish

Love is Born

Sauntering Lone

Kissing the Dew

Lonely

Gentle Rain

Angel Dance

Love Whispers

The Ark

Sleeping Melody

In Another Day

Chapters

The Struggle

Waiting For Your Kiss

Knowing You Care

Tears a Language

Ask His Son

Washed Ashore

A Mother's Prayer

Remembering You

Ring the Bells

Chapter 5

Bubbling Joy

Birthing Spring

The Story of My Love

I Can Hear

Heart's Path

A Supernatural Book

Broken Paths

The Journey

You've Got Mail

Forever My Love

Wind Whispers

I Close My Eyes to Dream

Shaking Rugs in the Rain (A Mother's Day Story)

Did You Hear That

Windowsill

Prism Bird

With God's Love

Butterfly Kisses

Flight of the Butterfly

The Meeting

Curb Side Shopping

A Poet Day

A Peter Pan Heart

Where Poems Grow

Nature Walk

Across The Sky

If These Walls Talked

We've Danced

Void of Words Immortal Hope

Making of a Star

Chapter 6

The Date

Take Time for Love

If I Were a Bird

Battle Song

Stephen & Persecution

Heaven's Place

Sandy's Run

The Writer's Muse

The Bride

I'm With You

White Drawn Sword and Silver Shield

Yours

Mirror, Mirror on the Wall

Another Fairytale

To The Market

True Love

A Father's Heart

The Lost

Sweet Love

At The End of the Aisle

Poet Dreaming

Through Eternities End

The Proposal

Love Glance

Blooming Love

White Splendor

She Met Him at the Picture Show

Reason Enough to Worry

Music

True Treasures

Chapter 7

Come Ride in my Car
Dream Away
One Hot Golden Brown French fry
Not About Games
Boot Camp for Heaven
Soothing Music
Whisper
Plastic Flower Never Die
Summer's Sun
Whispers of Aura
Build a Castle
Gossip
Rest Today
Lone Cloud
I May Never Write a Sonnet
By Faith
Steal My Heart
Gentle Spirit
Gentle Sea
The Visit
By Your Side
Whisper in my Ear
Sometimes I Don't Understand
My Obnoxious Little Fur
Bird of Prey
Live with Elvis
This is a Test
Mike's Black Angus Burger
Enchanted by the Muse
Going Home
Stage Fright

Chapter 8

I'll Meditate
Morning Games
Beyond Life's Path
Reflection of a Morning
The Church in the Cornfield
Somewhere Over the Rainbow
Path
Morning
The View
Folded Memory
Tommy Cat
God
Trippin' on the Train
The Date
Lost Song
Crossing
In the Shadow of Sunflowers
Dreams of Tomorrow
Be Encouraged
The Nightmare
Storm of the Heart
Where Angels Are Birthed
Listen to His Voice
Car Rider
Reflecting our Love
My Love
I Lift My Hands to You
Flying High
Sailing Through
Sleepless
Summer Love

Chapter 9

Sent From Above

Endless Heaven

Conflicting Thoughts

Another Day

The Keeper of the Keys

Poetry, Poetry

Pizza for Breakfast

A Troll

The Call

Hannah's Muse

Where Have All the Children Gone

Missing You Poet

Telephone Love

The Love of a Book

Rambling Thoughts

God's Essence

Birthing a Loving Cocoon

Faded Glory

My Heart Misses

Blink

A Fishy Tale

Touching Gift

Time

A Cinderella Dream

Whistling Blue Candy Man

Chapter 10

Glimpse of Heaven

Is There Any More

The Forbidden Fruit

The New Fall Season

Not a Puppet

Deaths by Frost

I Lift My Hands to You

Waiting For You to Ask

Iridescent Feather

My Shadow

The Novel

Rose on My Pillow

Empty Nest

Mustard Seed Faith

The Pumpkin

Yonder Where the Wheat Winds Blow

Be a Battleship

The Calling

Winter Whisper

The Fawn

Whisper a Prayer

Behind The Sunset

Sun Painting

Autumn

Early Morning

Shawn's Poem

The House on the Hill

He Came To Take You Back

Painting the Sunrise

Stumbled

Night of Dreams

Chapter 11

Walking the Sonlit Path

The First Bite

Breakfast Morning Out

Dawn the Day

Beyond The Sun

I Miss You

Demon Dark

The Armor

Fantasy World

Broken

Not Too Far Away

Rain Out Of My Window

Forever Yours

A Refreshing Fountain

The Fight

Amber's Poem

What Does It Take

Oh This Feeling, It's So Fine

The Legacy

The Music

Love All a Bed to Sleep

Thanksgiving the Unexpected Visitor

TV Oppression

Faith of the Mustard Seed

His Love

Reflection of a Dream

What a Day!

My Rock

Adoring Love

Chapter 12

Broken Wings

Enchanted Angels Sing

Sometimes My Halo Tilts a Bit

The Flight of the Snowflake

Lord Will See Me Through

Wars of Realms

Dried Roses

Note to God

Recycle

I Need You Near

Heart Yearn

Gift of Snow

The Vessel

I Hear Music

Alien under My Christmas tree

Guardian Angel

Deep

A Note from God

Saint Nicholas

A Poem for Misty

Together

The First Christmas

Why Is That Tune Stuck In My Head

Mary's Story

Child, Oh Child

Molding Vessels

But Never My Word

Wishing To Meet You

Burnt Out

Discouraged

The Last Page